The Plan That Broke the World

Books in this series
by *William D. O'Neil*

http://whatweretheythinking.williamdoneil.com/

What Were They *Thinking*?*
Bad Decisions—And How to Make Better Ones

The Plan That Broke the World
The "Schlieffen Plan" and World War I

Titanic Error*
How Titanic Sank Under the Weight of Bad Decisions

Undefending Pearl Harbor*
Why the World's Strongest Fortress Was Left Open to Attack

Building Black Holes*
The Channel Tunnel and the Space-Based Infrared System (SBIRS)

AIG and Enron*
Dysregulation, Dysfunction, and Destruction

* Not yet published as of February 2014

The Plan That Broke the World

The "Schlieffen Plan" and World War I

William D. O'Neil

Second edition
with revised introduction

Cover illustration:
Front: Poster by Egon Tschirch, *So säh' es aus in deutschen Landen, käm'
der Franzose an den Rhein*, lithograph 1918 by Verlag Selman Bayer, Berlin.
Back: C. R. W. Nevinson, *Column on the March*, oils, 1915.

whatweretheythinking.williamdoneil.com/theplanthatbroketheworld

Second edition with revised introduction

ISBN: 1481955853
ISBN-13: 978-1481955850

Contents

Figures

Acknowledgments

I COULDN'T EVEN BEGIN TO list all of the people who have provided research help or important insights and ideas that have shaped this book. There were many crucial things I needed to learn in order to write it and I'm very grateful for all the help I've had in learning them.

I do want to mention some members of a largely uncelebrated but absolutely essential group of people—research librarians and archivists. Rea Stone and more recently Linette Neal of the library at the Center for Naval Analyses (where I hold an appointment as a Senior Fellow) have been consistently responsive and helpful. And the Historical Office of the U.S. Army Communications-Electronics Command went to considerable trouble to provide essential material on early communications. Several others who prefer to remain anonymous also have been very helpful.

Sara-Ann Determan helped substantially with proofreading, an effort to which Scott Peterson also contributed.

Finally, I want to acknowledge the person whose consistent support, direct and indirect, has been most vital in this and all my work—my wife, Anne Murphy O'Neil.

1. Introduction

F EW PEOPLE TODAY CAN SEE much good in war, but World War I (1914–1918) has a particularly dreadful reputation. It's not only that the war was responsible for the deaths of 16 million people, mostly young and many by uniquely horrifying means, but its effects marked practically everyone who survived (at least in Europe and North America), and continue to torment us even after a century. There was nothing romantic or glorious in this war; it did vast harm and scarcely any good. Even the scanty benefits sometimes claimed for it are largely illusory.

The causes that underlie World War I seem grotesquely mysterious. Did Serbian leaders really launch one of the most ghastly wars in history by dispatching teenaged terrorists to shoot a widely-controversial Austrian prince and his wife on a dusty street in an obscure Balkan town? What can they have been *thinking*? What can leaders of other nations have been thinking when they piled on?

This book will briefly review the background of the war and the actions leading up to it, but it's really about why Germany's leaders in particular felt motivated to enter the war and to do so with an all-out invasion of France, by way of Belgium. They put their confidence in what's usually called the Schlieffen Plan, in honor of Count von Schlieffen, a former chief of the Prussian General Staff. Historian

John Keegan nominated it as "the most important official document of the last hundred years," anywhere.[1] Those with much interest in military history will usually tell you that it was the brilliant and audacious plan with which Germany began World War I in August 1914, intended to defeat the French Army in six weeks.

That's really quite wrong. Schlieffen played an important part in laying the groundwork for German war planning, but not the part that's usually described. And the plan that Germany was actually pursuing was only slightly like the one found in most books.

It's very frequently claimed that even though it led the German Empire to wreck and Europe to catastrophe, the plan was a work of genius that went awry only because it was botched by the men who executed it.[2] Yet even with the best possible execution the plan would have been far too risky for a bet-your-country wager. It wasn't the best of all possible plans, very far from it. The German Empire had realistic options for pursuing its objectives and needs with much lower risk, options that wouldn't have required knowledge, technology, or resources beyond what was available in the 1910s.

History is about what happened rather than what we imagine might have happened, but this book isn't really a history, or at least not primarily history. It explores the question of why very smart, well-prepared leaders made catastrophic miscalculations. To understand that we need to know what the alternatives were, not just the alternatives that they thought about and rejected but the ones they implicitly rejected without any thought, at least conscious thought.

Not many decisions go wrong on quite the same scale as those made by the leaders of Germany in late July of 1914, but major miscalculations aren't rare in human affairs. Studying German illusions at the start of World War I helps to illuminate not only the history of the war but what might be done to avert catastrophic miscalculations in the future.

· · ·

THE ULTIMATE PURPOSE of this book is to contribute to the exploration and understanding of the processes of large-scale decision-making, not to history itself. I'm not a professional historian and have done none of the original archival research that is the defining activity of professional historiography. But an accurate understanding of history is essential in order to understand how decision-making truly worked.

And that presents a problem. Even people who have devoted a fair amount of study to the First World War often have little knowledge of how and why the relevant decisions were made, nor of the circumstances that shaped and constrained them. And it's not as easy to find correct and relevant information as I had supposed when I started work on this book.

For the past four or five decades the substantial majority of the professional historians who've written about the war have focused most of their research on its "ordinary" people, those who bore most of its burdens, endured most of its hardships and privations, and did most of its bleeding and dying. It was of course the efforts of this mass of people, taken in sum, that ultimately determined the conflict outcomes and the fates of nations and peoples.

Nevertheless, the course of their efforts was guided and focused by the decisions (or indecisions) of a far smaller group of political and military leaders. Theirs is not the whole story and we cannot say even that it is the most important story in any absolute sense. But it's the important story for the purposes of this book, and that's the part of the history of the war that it deals with. Specifically, it deals with the decisions of Germany's military leadership about how to pursue their nation's war aims and how they related to the national decisions for war and the ways in which the decisions played out.

· · ·

EVEN THOUGH THIS is not a history book as such, it has a lot in it that will surprise many people who have read about the war. I know that because I've tried it on sample audiences and listened to their reactions. For most people, including many historians, World War I is a story of trench warfare and the spade is absent here. Many people are surprised to learn that Mons, Charleroi, the siege of Namur and the forcing of the Meuse above Namur are all names for various parts of one great battle, a battle usually recorded as a victory for the

German Army, but at which it lost what was surely its best opportunity to conclude the war on favorable terms.

There's also widespread lack of understanding of the state of
critical technologies in 1914, including motor vehicles, aircraft, electrical communications, and electronics. This isn't too surprising,
given how rapidly these technologies were moving at that time, but
it's important for the book's purposes to clarify their status.[*]

There has been great confusion regarding the so-called Schlieffen Plan and its role in how the war came about and Germany's ultimate failure to achieve her strategic aims. Reports of the plan's
nonexistence are much exaggerated, but serious misunderstandings
of what it was, how it came about and mutated, and how it related to
the actual operations of German armies in 1914 are common and often profound. The plan has to be seen for what it truly was in order
to understand why the German leaders acted as they did.

Many points made here are by no means new, but can be seen in
a new light. Arguments that Germany missed critical political, strategic, and technological opportunities were advanced by German
historians and military writers even before the guns had cooled, and
have reappeared periodically since. But important sources have been
published and explored in recent years and it is, ironically, easier in
many ways to assess the pre-war opportunities and perspectives objectively over the long term than it was from the opposite bank of
the war's gulf.

Much of what I've learned in the course of researching this book
has surprised me, and I've worked hard to ensure that it's right. I
have searched out strong sources and cross-checked critical points.

Although not trained as a professional historian I have other
qualifications of value. For a number of years I worked as a systems
engineer on a variety of defense-related developments and as a result
have in-depth understanding of the technological and technology-
application issues addressed here. And I also served as a planning
and operational intelligence officer on high-level military staffs, giv-

---

[*]   Chemical engineering also was progressing rapidly, and was very important
for the war overall, but didn't figure in the decisions of 1914 and before, although arguably it should.

ing me a good deal of insight into how staff planning and execution work in practice, as well as how commanders and staffs look at military problems. Finally I worked quite closely with a number of top-level government officials who were seeking to resolve policy problems relating to war and peace. (In many cases historians look at military and policy problems quite differently, and while this does not mean that they are wrong and the generals and officials are right it can tend to hinder their understanding of why generals and officials behaved as they did.)

These are not common background experiences for historians of World War I and they're essential to this book.

· · ·

THERE'S ONE ASPECT of the historical picture that I should say a few words about because it's particularly critical, obscure, and contentious: the responsibility for the war. For a great many people, probably a clear majority, it's a question with a very simple answer: The German Empire started the war in a quest to dominate Europe, after the fashion of Napoléon. Many respected historians hold it, with some variations and qualifications, and some of them (and many other people) take quite strong offense at any questioning of it.[3]

I present an alternative view of the origins of the war that seems to me more consistent with the evidence, on the whole. But it's not a subject about which there can be any ultimate certainty.

In any event, I take no position on the question of German "war guilt." I understand guilt as a moral category that cannot justly or meaningfully be applied to a nation, few of whose citizens had means to influence its actions or even accurate knowledge of what they were. There were plenty of Germans who had much to answer for, as there were individuals in almost all of the other countries involved, but this is a book about the process and foibles of decision; those who wish to pursue moral philosophy must look elsewhere.

The book argues that the Germans had it within their power to conduct the initial campaigns of the war more effectively and so to give themselves a better chance of achieving their fundamental political objectives—notably including the preservation of the German Empire. Some people may take this to mean that I think it would have been desirable for Germany to have prevailed in the war, but that's altogether wrong. The arguments are presented solely to clarify the extent to which the German high command failed to plan as wisely as it might. I certainly do not believe that the world would be better off if the Central Powers rather than the Allies had won the war. I do feel pretty sure that an early termination of the war on essentially a *status quo ante* basis would have been desirable but can see no particular value in arguing the point and have not written this book to do so.

. . .

I WRITE HERE ABOUT the foibles of German decision-making. That's important in itself, but it's also a part of a larger historical story, the failure of the German attempt to defeat France and her allies in the west in August and early September 1914.

While the German plan had important weaknesses (as detailed here) the German Army was stronger in almost every respect than any of the armies arrayed against it. It failed to defeat France and her two allies in the west, Belgium and Britain, in part because of the weaknesses of its planning but also in part because the allies did some important things right. Belgium had been terribly shortsighted and her army was much weaker than it might reasonably have been, but her sons were brave and in their courage and tenacity they sapped the German momentum significantly. Britain's small army achieved much less than it might have with even reasonably competent and active command but her troops did the best that the dismal quality of their leadership allowed and they too contributed greatly to sapping the momentum of the German right wing.

France played the key role. Her army suffered terribly from doctrinal muddle and from inadequate investment in development and training of her large reserve forces.[4] The supreme commander, Joseph Joffre, committed his forces to offensives based on a fundamental misreading of his opponent's capabilities and dispositions, with extremely costly results. Yet at the critical moment, late in August, Joffre recognized the reality and made exactly the move Germany's master planner, Schlieffen, had feared most—shifting major forces from his right wing to his left. This finally doomed German hopes of turning the allied left wing and enveloping the allied armies.

Perhaps even more important, virtually all of the allied commanders were alert to the need to pull back promptly when it became clear that the tide of battle was running against them. This may not seem like a major virtue but it was contrary to a fundamental assumption of German planning and made it impossible for the Germans to envelop and annihilate inferior forces. Thus the allied forces mostly survived to fight another day, and thanks to the resilience and courage of their troops were able to fight effectively.

. . .

WEIGHTY AS THE IMPLICATIONS of its subject may be, this has been framed as a very brief, readable book. There are occasional explanatory footnotes but the end-notes (indicated by superscript numerals) are strictly for reference sources; unless you want to know the source of something said in the text, or where you might look to learn more, you can safely ignore them entirely. While many sources have been consulted, I've tried to cite only the most relevant and accessible ones. Sources are cited in full at first use and in abbreviated form thereafter. The Bibliography gives full citations for all sources used more than once, and for other sources that played a significant part in the research, even if not specifically cited.

Because it's convenient sometimes to look at a map while reading text with geographic references and inconvenient to be flipping back and forth in the book, I've made a booklet of the maps available on the Web. This map booklet contains large, high-resolution, full-color PDF images of all of the maps from this book. It is solely for lawful owners and borrowers of *The Plan That Broke the World*, either in paper or electronic form. To download it go to:

http://williamdoneil.com/Plan_Maps/

There is a glossary of terms and abbreviations at page 187.

Personal names are mostly given in their native form and spelling. Many place names have alternative forms and I've tried to use the one that will be most familiar to English speakers, or the dominant local form when that didn't seem to be a consideration.

English forms have been used for most institutions, offices, etc., while native forms have been used for personal titles and ranks. Where applicable I've noted the English equivalents for native forms at first use and in the Glossary at the end of the book.

The caliber (bore diameter) of firearms is given in millimeters (with inch equivalents on first use). Terminology for artillery was varied (and sometimes intentionally deceptive); here any artillery piece that can fire at elevations from zero to no more than 50 degrees is referred to as a cannon, zero to more than 50 degrees as a howitzer, and no less than 45 degrees as a mortar.

Distances are in American statute miles (1609 m) or yards (0.91 m), weights in pounds (0.45 kg) and (short) tons (907 kg), and the power output of motors in horsepower (746 W).

States are referred to using feminine pronoun forms, a holdover from Latin that remains helpful in distinguishing them gracefully from institutions of other sorts.

My German was never fluent and since years of disuse have taken a further toll I've relied largely on translations, if only because professional translators are more likely to penetrate to the real meaning than I. A number of the sources in the notes and bibliography are translated from the German. Even though English and German share common linguistic roots, translation between them is by no means straightforward and there is a risk of serious misunderstandings. Wherever possible I have cross-checked key points across various independent sources; in a few instances I've very carefully translated key passages myself to be sure.

The book's Web site at

whatweretheythinking.williamdoneil.com/theplanthatbroketheworld

has a variety of supplementary information.

The Web site for the overall series at

whatweretheythinking.williamdoneil.com/

explains its unifying concept and provides further links.

11.Prussia and Empire

BEFORE THERE WAS GERMANY THERE was a multitude of Germanies, small states speaking more or less the same language and clustered more or less across the midriff of Europe between the Baltic Sea to the Adriatic.

Until the mid–1800s the largest and strongest of these was Austria, politically dominated by Germans but ruling over other peoples speaking other languages, mostly Hungarians and Slavs of various kinds but also including a number of smaller ethnic groups. From the 1700s, however, a late starter had been closing on Austria: Prussia. Before the latter 1600s she'd been a minor state in the north, with little land, population, wealth or strength, subject to the whims of her larger and stronger neighbors. But by the time that Prussia's Frederick the Great (*Friedrich II*, 1712–1786; r. 1740–1786) died in 1786 his nation had become the fifth of Europe's five generally recognized Great Powers (along with France, Austria, Russia and Britain).[1]

Great Power status was a good thing, for it meant that other Great Powers couldn't simply ignore your interests. In the Europe of the 1700s and 1800s it meant that when there was pie to be divided you could claim your piece. But to keep your seat at the pie-carving table you had to be ready to defend it. And Prussia was fighting above her weight—she had only the thirteenth largest population and tenth greatest land area in Europe even after the conquests of Frederick the Great. It was the strength of his armies rather than her size that made Prussia's power Great.[2]

Along with almost all of the states of Continental Europe, Prussia fell before the onslaught of Napoléon I, Emperor of the French (1769–1821; r. 1804–1814, 1815). Her turn came in 1806, and Napoléon was careful to keep her under his heel. But his defeat in the disastrous Russian campaign of 1812 gave the Prussians room to reconstitute their army and join other Great Powers in the final efforts to defeat him. This gained Prussia a seat at the Congress of Vienna, convened to stitch Europe back together again after Napoléon had been sent off to the early 1800s equivalent of Guantánamo Bay, the isolated island of St. Helena. She wasn't reckoned as being quite as Great a Power as Russia, Austria or Britain, and didn't get all that her leaders wanted or thought they deserved, but Prussia emerged from the wheelings and dealings in Vienna in a stronger position than she had held before the wars, stronger even than her leaders understood.

In 1789 there had been 365 German-speaking states or portions of states gathered in an extremely loose "Holy Roman Empire" normally reigned over by the Austrian monarch. Napoléon had swept it all away and the Congress of Vienna had reconstituted a "mere" 40 states and territories joined in a nearly powerless German Confederation under Austrian leadership. Prussia didn't like it, but lacked the power to do anything about it.

Like almost all the countries of Europe, Prussia was battered by the storm of revolutionary movements in 1848. She rode it out better than many, but the monarch was forced to grant the country's first constitution, establishing a Parliament (*Landtag*) with power over raising money.

And the Prussian state needed money. Railroads were transforming Europe and especially Prussia, where they promised economical transport for the grain that was still the country's main export, and the government wanted an active hand in building them to maximize economic benefit and military value. The army was antiquated and unready, so if Prussia's policy was not to be the cat's-paw of larger states she needed more military strength.

As a further complication, in 1857 the then-King was incapacitated by a stroke and his brother was made regent, assuming the throne four years later as King Wilhelm I (1797–1888; r. 1861–1888) when the childless monarch died. He had spent his life in the army, starting as a pre-teen cadet in the wars against Napoléon. Little in his experience or sketchy education had prepared him for dealing with a recalcitrant parliament in a volatile political environment and he often despaired of the task.

The man who sustained and steadied him was an old friend, comrade and confidant whom he had appointed as Minister of War, General Albrecht von Roon (1803–1879).[*] Roon was profoundly conservative and had no love at all for popular government. But he was a realist and had a younger friend whom he thought might bend events to his will: Otto von Bismarck (1815–1898), a brilliant young conservative whose fiery ideas alarmed even other conservatives.[3]

. . .

FOR A YEAR after his accession Wilhelm resisted Roon's advice and tried to rely on more "reasonable" ministers. But by 1862 he felt that the time had come for desperate measures and called Bismarck to be his Prime Minister (*Ministerpräsident*) as well as Foreign Minister.

Bismarck had scarcely any friends in Parliament nor any base of popular support. All he had was the support of the King, and that at first was limited and tentative. He kept his post because no one could find an alternative, dealing with Parliament as he would a recalcitrant horse, with whip and spurs. But in the longer term he realized something more positive was needed.

Pan-German nationalism was growing rapidly, demanding national unification. Bismarck despised nationalists of all kinds as romantic fools but decided to exploit the power of the movement to advance Prussia. Through a series of three "Wars of Unification" between 1864 and 1871 he built domestic support in Prussia while con-

---

[*]   The "von" before Roon's name indicated membership in the aristocracy. He later was granted the title of *Graf* (count), but as simply a *von* he was roughly the social equivalent of a squire, knight or baronet in England.

solidating the kingdom's power. In each case he concocted high-minded rationales for conflicts he largely initiated and controlled.

First came a war against Denmark. Prussia and Austria fought side by side in the name of the German Confederation over the issue of who lawfully merited the right to rule the provinces of Schleswig and Holstein. After that was done and the Danes driven back, Bismarck engineered a conflict with Austria, which to general European astonishment Prussia won in a matter of weeks in 1866. Bismarck's peace terms re-drew the map of Germany and required Austria to withdraw from German affairs. The results in geographic terms are shown in the middle panel of Figure 2.

**Figure 1. King Wilhelm I rides out to war in 1870,
followed by Bismarck, the elder Moltke, and Roon.[4]**

TRIUMPHS BROUGHT BISMARCK POPULARITY among many, and fearful respect elsewhere. He consolidated his power as he sought the right opportunity. In 1870 he contrived to maneuver and goad the French Emperor Napoléon III into attacking. (Napoléon III (1808–1873; r. 1852–1870) was the nephew of Napoléon I; he had slipped into power in the turmoil following the 1848 revolution.) Germans everywhere remembered that the Emperor's uncle had conquered and humiliated their nation six decades earlier and practically everyone harbored a burning nationalistic hostility toward France. All the German states, even those not under Bismarck's direct control, joined in.

Combined under Prussian command, the German armies made very short work of the French Army, widely thought to have been Europe's strongest. Within just 45 days the coalition army defeated the great bulk of the French forces and took them prisoner, along with Napoléon III himself. French politicians who had long chafed under his Second Empire proclaimed a revived republic and swore resistance to the invader. A great tide of patriotic fervor carried hundreds of thousands of volunteers forward to improvise new armies. There were months of bitter struggle but the amateurish newly-raised forces could make no progress against the Germans and in the end France capitulated.

As Bismarck had calculated, triumph over her old enemy had left Germany at last ready for unification. With gleaming promises, silken threats and shadowy bribes the kings, princes, and heads of the remaining 28 independent German states were all induced to sign a treaty-constitution subordinating themselves to the Prussian King in his new role as German Emperor.

But how was the new state to be governed? The new constitution was silent or ambiguous on many crucial points, with little central governmental mechanism and very limited central government power. That had been essential to gain agreement but it didn't make a strong basis for the state.

As the godlike architect of German unification, Bismarck was for a time able to govern fairly effectively, but the magic soon faded. Divisions within the new Empire went deep enough that he couldn't possibly span them all, especially not while retaining ultimate power.

Bismarck was most noted for his mastery of foreign relations. Prussia's victories against Austria and France had been possible only because he had successfully isolated Prussia's foes diplomatically and ensured that none of the other Great Powers would intervene against Prussia. He played on their fears, ambitions and jealousies, paying them off (usually at someone else's expense) and balancing one against another.[5]

Figure 2. Prussia to Empire, 1820–1871.[6]

After the defeat of France he turned to ensuring the security of the new Empire he had called into existence. The victory and the peace terms Prussia had dictated had created a permanent threat in the hostility and resentment of the defeated. The searing symbol of German injustice was Alsace-Lorraine, a broad strip of territory ripped from eastern France—visible in the bottom frame of Figure 2. The Prussian Army's leaders (and the King) had insisted on it to strengthen Germany's defenses, but at the same time the annexation greatly exacerbated the threat.

Although it had greater military potential than Prussia ever could mobilize, the strategic position of Bismarck's new German Empire was problematic, bordered on three sides by great powers whose interests could conflict with Germany's: Russia, Austria-Hungary,[*] and France. Prussia had generally good relations with Russia and Austria in the 1800s, notwithstanding some conflicts, and although there was periodic friction with Britain nothing threatened war.

From the standpoint of German security the rupture with France was a wound that could not heal. France's population was smaller than Germany's—and growing more slowly—so there was little prospect that France could gather the strength to defeat her northeastern neighbor by herself. But if France were to combine with another Great Power then Germany could come into real danger, facing war on two or more borders. Thus the continuing isolation of France had to be a fixed objective of German policy.

Bismarck made a defensive alliance with Austria-Hungary and a more limited one with Russia, while avoiding friction with France and Britain. But having lost most of her German and Italian territories and interests the Dual Monarchy was turning toward the Bal-

---

[*]   Following Austria's defeat by Prussia in 1866 the Hungarian half had won semi-independence within the empire with its own parliament and government that was autonomous in Hungarian affairs. The result became known as the Austro-Hungarian Empire, often called the Dual Monarchy or Habsburg Monarchy—for the Habsburg family that held the thrones both of Austria and Hungary.

kans, where the Ottoman Empire of the Turks was losing its grip on power.

Figure 3. Bismarck, 1870 and 1881.

The other major power bordering the Balkans was Russia, with emotional connections to the region's many Slavic peoples reinforcing more material interests. If the Balkans were to be dominated by Russia or even Russian-aligned local powers, the men in Vienna reasoned, their empire would be in great danger. For the sake of her own security Germany had to be sure that she kept both Vienna and St. Petersburg* on her side. But how could this be possible if they were on course for a collision?

---

*   St. Petersburg, not Moscow, was then the Czar's capital.

III. Prussia's Military System

PRUSSIA'S VULNERABLE GEOSTRATEGIC POSITION AND determination to run with the Great Powers despite smaller size and lesser resources had compelled special attention to war and maximizing warmaking potential at the lowest price. While it's wrong to say, as some have, that Prussian "militarism" was the central cause of World War I, the nation's unique military system had a pervasive effect.[1]

Prussia's military system both reflected and was reflected in her society as a whole. One of the nation's enduring distinctive features was particular attention to education and intellectual excellence; much of modern science and engineering have Prussian roots. Such a country would naturally nurture and rely on intellectual soldiers.

The capstone institution of Prussian military intellectualism was the General Staff (*der Generalstab*). Every major command had its own general staff with one or more qualified officers of the General Staff but at the head was the Great (or Central) General Staff (*der großer Generalstab*). Assignment to the GGS was a prize won through a rigorous and demanding process of selection and education, with rewards that included increased opportunities for promotion and high command as well as the absorbing challenge of intense involvement in the central nervous system of the Army.[2]

Napoléon had the largest and most efficient staff of his day, but he'd been his own master planner and relied on the staff primarily for quick and efficient development and execution of the details to support his fluid vision. But other innovations of the Napoleonic era and subsequently would increasingly challenge this approach and lead the GGS to gradually develop and implement fundamental modifications.

The wars of the French Revolution and Empire had summoned armies of previously unimaginable size to European battlefields. At the largest battle of the wars more than half a million men fought. To raise huge armies France had developed a system of near-universal conscription; opponents had little choice but to follow.

Mass citizen armies, with their overtones of popular power, were viewed with suspicion and hostility by autocratic regimes, most of which gladly reverted to restricted recruitment and long-service professional armies after Napoléon was gone. Even Napoléon III, who tried hard to ride on his uncle's glorious coattails in every possible way, avoided conscript armies. But with a comparatively small population and looming threats, Prussia's elites felt that they had no choice but to retain and refine wide-scale conscription.

Mixing practices from the past with the French conscription system they developed a hybrid that would transform European warfare and dominate for a century and half. Every year a substantial portion of the young men turning 20 (but never close to all of them in peacetime) would be conscripted. They would serve on active duty for two or three years (the period varied from time to time and branch to branch), providing a standing force while they received intensive training. Then they transferred to the reserve, where they periodically took several weeks of training to maintain their skills. This permitted Prussia to expand the Army to several times its peacetime strength on very short notice when needed while not imposing burdens the country could not bear.

Several measures were taken to assure the political reliability of this mass army. Conscription was concentrated in rural areas, away from the restless and disturbing influence of the cities, and recruits of proven ability and loyalty could become noncommissioned officers (NCOs), a major route to upward economic and social mobility, with the reward of a government job after retirement. Candidates for commissioned officer rank were drawn from educated young men with strong incentives for loyalty to king and country, especially the sons of the nobility and higher civil service.

By the time of the Austro-Prussian War Prussia put armies of more than 200,000 in the field, ten times those of a century earlier. While Frederick the Great had been able to maneuver his forces with relative freedom, the larger armies of the late 1800s had grown unwieldy due to their sheer size compared to the scale of the countryside and road networks, and especially compared to the distance that men could march in a few hours. In the course of a day the rear guard of a mass so large could not reach the positions that had been occupied by the advance guard at dawn, even marching in multiple columns on parallel roads. A bulky mass moving so slowly simply could not be turned quickly, any more than an inchworm—it's a geometric impossibility. New patterns and organizations needed to be developed

Napoléon and his opponents had transferred large armies across Europe on foot, but only with weeks or months of delay. The new railroads offered a far better alternative. While trains could be used for tactical deployments only in particularly favorable circumstances, and while an army advancing into hostile territory was likely to find rail routes blocked to it, railroads had the potential to mass forces very rapidly at selected points on the frontier.

Weapons technology was also changing. Napoléon's troops had fought with smoothbore muzzle-loading flintlock muskets and cannon using similar technology. Rates of fire were low, ranges short and accuracy poor. Mid-century weapons still were muzzle-loaded, but rifling had considerably improved range and accuracy, while use of percussion caps in place of flintlocks permitted some increase in the rate and reliability of fire. Soon breech-loading started to come into use, greatly increasing firing rates. The first machine guns appeared in the 1860s.[3]

Battlefields grew far more deadly and far larger. The bayonet charges of the earlier wars, with troops advancing in ranks across

200 yards or more of open ground, became exercises in self-immolation. Columns couldn't move within several miles of the enemy without coming under artillery fire, greatly limiting maneuver possibilities.

Unless something were done these changes would disproportionately favor the defense, making it impossible to achieve rapid victory. To Prussian strategists this threatened the nation's fundamental security. Prussia, small and limited in resources, couldn't sustain a war lasting years as Russia or France might they feared. If a larger power threatened it had to be rebuffed swiftly and decisively before Prussia could be worn down. To accomplish this the Army had to carry the fight to the enemy and with no more than a handful of sharp blows definitively rebuff the threat.[4] Prussian strategists saw this as the story of both the Austro-Prussian and Franco-Prussian Wars.

To be sure, to others both conflicts looked like wars of aggression, fought not to protect Prussia from threats but to advance her policy aims. It's hard to believe that Bismarck didn't share this view but the official line, in the Army at least, was that it had only been defending the homeland. The dichotomy did little to increase trust in Prussian (and later German) intentions. But for whatever objectives the GGS felt it had to recapture the potential to inflict swift and irreversible defeat on enemies.

In 1857 the General Staff got a new chief, Helmuth von Moltke*(1800–1891), often referred to as Moltke the Elder to distinguish him from his nephew and namesake who also plays a central part in our story.[5] He was early recognized for his high intellectual qualities and served in a variety of General Staff appointments. At the same time he made himself welcome in court and gained appointment as aide-de-camp to a young prince (and future king). When the King was stricken by a stroke in 1857 the young prince's father, Prince Wilhelm, became regent; one of his first acts was to appoint Moltke to replace a veteran of the wars with Napoléon who had just died in office as the GGS chief.[6]

---

* In 1870 Moltke was created *Graf* (equivalent to *Count* in English) and is often identified as Helmuth Graf von Moltke, or simply Graf Moltke.

Moltke paid special attention to railroads and under his direction the GGS formulated plans for mobilizing and concentrating the army by rail.[7] By the time of the war with Denmark in 1864 Moltke's planning and Roon's material improvements had brought gains. But getting commanders to implement Moltke's ideas in the field remained a problem. In 1866, at the outset of the Austro-Prussian War, Moltke was given the authority as chief of the GGS to issue orders in the King's name, making him in effect the commander in chief of the Prussian Army.

Figure 4. Moltke the Elder. *

CONSISTENT WITH PRUSSIA'S fundamental strategic objective, Moltke sought to "annihilate" the enemy in one battle or rapid succession of battles. *Annihilate* not necessarily in the sense of wholesale slaughter but of rendering the enemy thoroughly impotent to further stand in Prussia's way. This of course wasn't novel; annihilation of this sort had always been Napoléon's objective as well—and Alexander the Great's, for that matter. Many other commanders, however, had congratulated themselves on great victories which had accomplished little more than leaving them in possession of the field. For Prussia it

---

*   The medal at his throat, which will be seen in other photos here, is the *Pour le Mérite*, Prussia's highest decoration for merit, established by Frederick the Great.

was essential to do more than force the enemy to retreat and re-group.[8]

Like Napoléon, Moltke took the corps as the basic formation of large-scale maneuver. By 1914 a German corps consisted of two divisions plus added support and logistics units, totaling roughly 42,500 troops plus 14,000 horses and 2,400 horse-drawn wagons at full war strength.[9] Marching as compactly as possible along a good road the corps stretched 30 miles and more, so it normally advanced no more than half its length in the course of a day. Even the pure combat forces stretched out a minimum of 15 miles so that if the lead elements met the enemy it would take a day of hard marching to fully deploy the corps for combat.[10] Thus a corps represented the strongest element of force compact enough to be moderately maneuverable. Two or (usually) more corps united with additional support and logistics units could be grouped under a field army.

Railroad trains running on schedules planned very precisely well in advance delivered mobilized corps to concentration areas near the frontiers. From there they formed up and marched forward by foot to engage the enemy along parallel roads, separated to avoid congestion and permit rapid advance. But as they reached the enemy they maneuvered to place a portion of the force at the front of the enemy with the rest on one or both of his flanks, poised to cut off his line of retreat. A determined frontal attack it was believed, even by a weaker force, would prevent the enemy from maneuvering or slipping away while the flanking forces closed in for the kill. If all went according to plan he would be caught between two attacks and shattered, annihilated as an effective fighting force.

It was a tricky recipe to carry out. As Moltke repeatedly emphasized, nothing in war is entirely foreseeable or ever goes according to plan. At best, the top commander maneuvered his forces into advantageous positions, and then it was up to subordinate commanders all down the line to meet the challenges of the moment as best they could. Trying to do it all with intricate, rigidly precise plans guaranteed chaos and failure, Moltke insisted.

The war plan was really a plan for the initial deployment, with a broad concept for subsequent operations. Ideally it accounted for what was susceptible to accounting, but for all else offered only concepts and guidance. It minutely laid out how the forces mobilized by local Army commands were to be transported to concentration areas, chiefly by rail, and how they were to concentrate and be readied to advance. Beyond that it was necessary to adjust frequently in response to ever-changing conditions and needs.

Every day on campaign, after movement and combat had wound down for the night, the commanders of the field armies were to report on the day's events and the prospects for the morrow to the Supreme Army Headquarters. After the Chief of Staff digested these reports along with intelligence and reconnaissance reports and the advice of his staff he issued orders on the Kaiser's behalf for the following day's operations. This pattern was followed in all the subordinate levels of command, corps reporting to their field army commanders, divisions to their corps commanders, etc.

The orders could never be complete and couldn't cover all contingencies. The commander could only call the plays; it was up to his subordinates to know how to execute them, come what may, guided by what a modern-day soldier knows as doctrine. To the soldier, doctrine is a guide not to belief but to action. It's a set not of recipes but of principles, and although there usually is an effort to write them down they must become innate and internalized to be fully effective. Ideally doctrine transforms a set of scattered individuals with limited communications into an integrated action network, each member knowing what is expected in any given situation and what can be expected of others.

The web of doctrine stretched from the private soldier all the way to the Chief of the Army General Staff (as the GGS chief became in wartime) and was spun by multiple spiders. Its lower reaches were the responsibility of the War Minister and of the commanders of the peacetime corps, while its apex belonged to the chief of the GGS. He developed and communicated it through a yearly round of exercises in the field (some with troops and others with commanders and staffs alone) together with a variety of war games in and near the GGS headquarters in Berlin.

Putting higher-level doctrine into effect was the principal duty of the officers of the General Staff. Every division, corps, and field army headquarters had its own general staff with one or more General Staff officers whose duty was not only to carry out the directions of its commander but to ensure that they meshed with doctrine.

Prussian doctrine—which in effect became the doctrine of the German Army as a whole—placed great stress on flexibility, imagination, and daring. While recklessness was not acceptable, commanders and General Staff officers were encouraged and expected to take calculated risks where there were rewards to be gained, recognizing that this would sometimes lead to defeat rather than victory. Passivity and inactivity were never the right answer; while some situations called for defense rather than attack it should be an active defense.

If possible without losing the initiative, Moltke recommended taking advantage of the tactical strength of the defensive stance as part of the offensive scheme, swiftly occupying some vital point the enemy was compelled to attack. Once he had worn himself out Prussian forces could take the offensive.

While his doctrine never worked exactly as it was supposed to, Moltke nevertheless was marvelously successful. Prussia won three wars in less than a decade and went from the second power in the Germanies to the master of all of Germany, save only Austria—which she had pushed into a second-class position. Modern armchair generals may criticize Moltke in the light of the accumulated experience of more than a century, but in his day he was better than anyone he fought against, and that's what counts most in war.

Everyone wanted to emulate Moltke and Prussia. But replicating success is not as easy as it may sound; there's always a secret sauce. Otherwise the world would overflow with Googles and Amazons and Apples, and Nepal would be as prosperous as Switzerland. Prussia's military system grew out of a particular social, political, economic, and geographic situation and could not be exactly replicated elsewhere.

So everyone adopted a general staff and a conscription system, and built railroads to deploy troops rapidly as well as staff colleges to train officers. Armies everywhere copied Prussian styles in drill, uniforms, and moustaches. And no one got quite the same results.

There's a lot of woolly talk about German superiority on the battlefield. It was very real but not a matter of some innate racial aptitude.[11] For more than two centuries, since the late 1600s, warmaking potential had been a major priority for Prussia (and to a lesser extent for the other principal German states). The social and political structures of the state had been adapted to support it to an extent duplicated nowhere else. In addition, Prussians were especially literate and tended to put a particularly high emphasis on individual responsibility and achievement. As a result young Prussian men were well prepared not just to be very dutiful soldiers but to be intensively trained so that they would be capable of executing complex tactical doctrine requiring not only courage but presence of mind and initiative on the highly stressful battlefield.

Prussia led in creating the social and economic conditions—and political structure—to produce a strong cadre of well-qualified non-commissioned officers to conduct immediate hands-on training of recruits, as well as lead them in small units in battle. No other state had nearly enough well-qualified NCOs, yet without them it was impossible to realize the potential offered by good soldier material.[12] And nations to Germany's east and south, including Russia, Italy, the Balkan states and much of Austria-Hungary, were handicapped by lower levels of social and educational development among most conscripts.

Finally, Prussia had created especially strong incentives for able young men to take up careers as military officers, and the means to select and educate those with the greatest gifts of intellectual ability and drive to provide planning and direction. Crucially, she had done this without imperiling the state. In fact the close alignment between the objectives of the Army and the state was the fundamental reason that Prussia was thought of as a "militarized" country. It was a path other Europeans feared to tread but their reluctance complicated their search for military strength to match Germany's.

While Europe and the world lauded and sought to imitate the elder Moltke, the aging master himself was as always rethinking his ideas in the light of experience and events, and coming to some disturbing conclusions. Thanks not only to his abilities and German military efficiency but also to the ineptness of the French command, his forces had annihilated their Army in just over six weeks in 1870, achieving the military objective. Yet the war machine continued to grind for another eight months as France raised new forces, costing many of Germany's casualties. If Bismarck had not held off other powers by diplomacy, Germany, with her forces tied down in France, could have been in danger.[13]

Immediately afterward, even before peace was concluded, Moltke declared that in the event of a two-front war,

> Germany cannot hope to rid herself of one enemy by a quick offensive victory in the West in order then to turn against the other. We have just seen how difficult it is to bring even the victorious war against France to an end.[14]

As France recovered and rearmed far more quickly than anyone had foreseen, and as French leaders demanded *revanche*, Moltke spoke of preemptive war to somehow finally guarantee Germany's security. But after weighing the issues at much greater length he warned that

> [If] war breaks out, then its duration and its end will be unforeseeable. ... [I]t may be a war of seven years' or of thirty years' duration....[15]

In short, for Germany to start another European war would be an act of awful, self-destructive folly—this according to the man acclaimed as the greatest soldier of his age.

IV. In the Reign of the Last Kaiser

IN 1887 WILHELM I REMAINED on the throne, Bismarck continued as his Chancellor, and the elder Moltke still was Chief of his Great General Staff. It was all much as it had been a quarter of a century earlier, all that many Prussians had ever known. Wilhelm I celebrated his 90th birthday in 1887, but didn't live out another year. His soldier-son, succeeding as Kaiser Friedrich III (1831–1888), was already mortally ill. After his 99-day reign the Prussian and Imperial throne passed to his own first-born son, Wilhelm II (1859–1941, r. 1888–1918).

The 29-year old monarch presented a dynamic contrast to his nonagenarian grandfather. He was intelligent, educated, personable, and gifted in the modern arts of promotion and popular public speaking. The young Emperor was ambitious to lead Germany to the heights of political, economic, and military greatness. But he was seriously affected with what we would today call attention deficit hyperactivity disorder (ADHD), perhaps as a result of the same birth trauma that stunted and largely paralyzed his left arm, and he never concentrated sustained attention on any of the great problems of state.[1]

Wilhelm's relationships with his parents had been tortured and unsatisfying, particularly with his mother. As Emperor he gathered around him an inner court of intimates who fawned on him and offered themselves to be the butt of his often cruel and demeaning pranks in return for royal access and patronage. In every situation Wilhelm was strongly driven to dominate.

Figure 5. Picture of grandiosity. State portrait at start of Wilhelm II's reign.[2]

The old monarch, Wilhelm I, had been willing, if not always glad, to allow Bismarck to govern largely as he saw fit in the name of the monarchy, but Wilhelm's grandson and namesake had his own ideas and chafed at the chancellor's imperiousness. After several clashes, the young Kaiser forced Bismarck out in 1890, a fortnight before his 75th birthday.

Although there was a personal element in Bismarck's dismissal, fundamental differences in policy also played a role. Bismarck had taken high risks to build a Prussian-led German Empire. But once it was established he focused on its security and internal growth, spurning all diversions. He spun a web of mutual interests and obligations with every major European state but France, binding them to support Germany's security—and even with France he was able to build calm if not warm relations. He had done all he could to establish Germany's image as a reliable, steady, reasonable Great Power, a state that could be depended upon to play by the rules.

This was far too cautious for Wilhelm and his advisors. Germany was a great and powerful empire that no one would dare challenge and there was no reason why it shouldn't elbow its way to the head of every line it chose, even at the price of some bruised feelings. That was the way of Great Powers, they thought, not timid obsession with good relations and security. They imagined that they were simply looking at things realistically.

Bismarck had negotiated a very limited alliance with Russia, the so-called Reinsurance Treaty, which expired soon after his dismissal. It was a needless restriction on Germany's freedom of action in the eyes of the man Wilhelm II had appointed in Bismarck's place, and he refused to renew it. The French sought to fill the gap by allying themselves with Russia. It was a tense match, republican and anti-monarchical France with autocratic and anti-republican Russia, but France offered major military and development aid and other incentives to help close the deal.

The failure to renew the Reinsurance Treaty is usually cited as a great diplomatic blunder, opening the way to close Franco-Russian ties that directly threatened Germany. Bismarck himself had put obstacles in renewal's path when for domestic political purposes he had pursued trade and tariff wars with Russia. It's also true that the treaty failed to address some of Russia's most pressing security concerns.[3] Nevertheless the slashing of the tie with Russia was probably something whose danger Bismarck would have foreseen and contrived to avoid, or at very least tried to.

Also very dangerous in the long run was Germany's rupture with Britain. Britain was unique among the European Great Powers in having no land frontiers bordering any other Power. Her navy was the world's most powerful, but her army was small and oriented entirely toward colonial wars. Since Germany was a land power with little real need of naval power Britain posed no direct military threat to her. Yet many Germans felt consumed with envy of Britain's wealth and position in the world, and impelled to compete with the British in every possible way.[4]

In fact following Britain's early lead in industrialization and science, Germany's wealth and trade surged ahead in the period before World War I. There was every prospect that she would supplant Britain in economic leadership, and soon come to dominate an increasingly integrated Europe. But it wasn't enough for some German leaders, including the Kaiser, who led the nation into policies that corroded relations with Britain without major gain for Germany.

To German surprise, Britain found her economic and colonial interests compatible with those of France, her ancient rival. Combined with their mutual imperial security concerns this led to a somewhat loose but real alliance, the *Entente Cordiale*. On its face it was simply a scheme for dividing up colonial spheres of interest, but since Germany had colonial aspirations herself it could not avoid an implicit anti-German coloration. Furthermore in 1907 Britain and Russia composed their longstanding colonial differences in Asia and the Middle East in another division of spheres of influence, also implicitly freezing Germany out. This was largely a result of St. Petersburg's awareness of Russia's weakness following its disastrous 1904–1905 war with Japan. Nevertheless, without formal alliance, Britain entered into a tacit *Triple Entente* with France and Russia. Nothing was guaranteed regarding Europe but it opened paths of friendly communication and recognition of mutual interest. While top officials were firm and explicit that there was no British commitment to intervene in a conflict, they permitted secret periodic discussions of defense problems between the French General Staff and their own. There were no similar British-Russian talks but the French and Russian staffs did confer and make definite common plans and commitments.

Thus Germany found herself facing the distinct possibility of a tight British blockade of her foreign trade in event of war with France and Russia. Moreover, with colonial threats abating and European ties growing, the British Army began to prepare itself for war on the Continent. While Britain's army was small and limited in its capabilities, she had the population and wealth to raise strong armies given some time, as she frequently had earlier. So the *Triple Entente* heightened the urgency of concluding any war quickly, before Germany could be ground down. Against the Entente stood the Triple Alliance, uniting Germany with Austria-Hungary and Italy. Unfortunately for Germany, neither of her alliance partners was especially strong—and Italy was not very faithful.

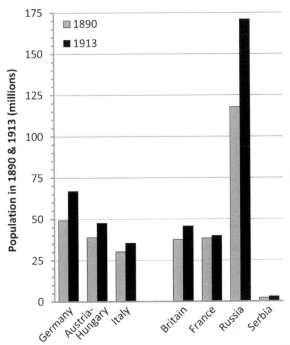

Figure 6. Population comparisons.[5]

The choices that nations had made before World War I were strongly influenced by perceptions of relative strength and threat. These perceptions in turn were influenced (but not directly determined) by statistical facts and Figures 6 through 9 show some indicators of strength.

The populations of the various states are shown in Figure 6, giving an indication of relative potential military manpower as well as potential productive labor. Figures both for 1890 and 1913 are shown to give an idea of growth. Germany was well in advance of Britain in growth, and far ahead of France. But Russia dwarfed them all both in the absolute size of her population and its growth. Although Austria-Hungary's area was great, much of it was uninviting terrain with little population.

What Figure 6 omits of course is any indication of how productive the people in various lands were in terms of agricultural and industrial output.

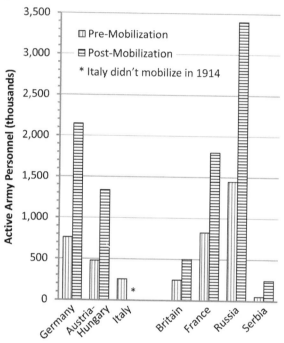

Figure 7. Army strength comparisons.[6]

Russia's large and rapidly-growing population gave the *Triple Entente* a potential edge in military manpower, as long as Russia could convert raw manpower into effective fighting strength. An idea of how many troops each combatant maintained before the war and how many each mustered to the colors in August 1914 is given by Figure 7. Peacetime strengths were pretty widely known but there were some surprises about mobilized strengths—not so much in total numbers as in the proportion truly fit for front-tine combat. Here Germany gained a strong advantage through superior training, doctrine and equipment—all made possible by her level of economic development. France conscripted a larger portion of her population, but was not able to make them as efficient as troops. Russia's forces were huge, but severely handicapped in training, doctrine and (to a somewhat lesser degree) equipment.

The level of competence of the top Russian commanders was poor for the most part and their performance was further undermined by political feuds among them. The officers of the Russian General Staff spent most of their time on routine and were much less well prepared than their German counterparts. The officer corps was handicapped by a wide range of serious social problems and remarkably lax professional standards. And the Russian Army suffered seriously from lack of enough good NCOs. This isn't to say that the Russians were negligible but they weren't nearly as strong as raw manpower suggested, nor as many in Europe imagined.[7]

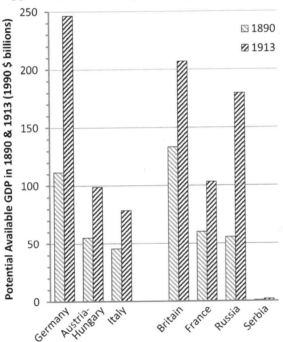

Figure 8. Economic strength comparisons.[8]

Leaders were alert to various indicators of economic capacity. Figure 8 sums it up in terms of output in 1913, after deducting $500 per person to allow for minimum subsistence needs.* Comparable figures for 1890 give an idea of output growth. Germany, combining rapid industrialization and growing population, led France and Britain—a subject of much agonizing in France and some in Britain. But Germans looked warily eastward, where Russia's growth was faster yet. This was in part the result of several years of unusually good harvests but industrialization, long delayed, was finally starting to take hold in the land of the czars.

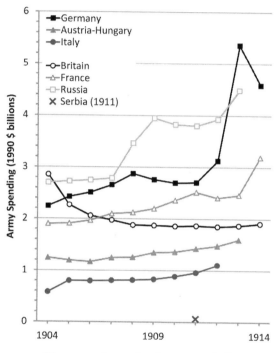

Figure 9. Army budget trends.[9]

Finally, Figure 9 shows trends of army budgets in the final years of peace. Accounting for military budgets was complex and arcane almost everywhere and various sources present widely varying results, so these figures need to be viewed cautiously. The figures shown were publicly available at the time.

---

* Like other economic values here this has been calculated on the basis of 1990 dollars using purchasing power parities for that year. Values in 2010 dollars would be roughly 70 percent greater, so the subsistence allowance would translate to about $850.

The big bulge in Russia's army spending after 1907 was less significant than it looks. First, it very largely went to rebuild an army shattered by its multiple defeats in the 1904–1905 war with Japan over Manchuria. Second, much of it represented money lent by French bankers (with strong government encouragement). Finally, the chaos and corruption of government finances undermined the ability to mobilize resources, while the unsophistication and inefficiency of Russia's newly emergent defense industry combined with erratic direction from a venal and divided top leadership and widespread corruption to erode what her army got for the money it spent on matériel and supplies.[10] When Russia decided on war in 1914 her army was seriously short of ammunition and matériel.[11]

British spending too is somewhat distorted by recovery from the Boer War in the early years of this period. Subsequently Britain spent on bringing equipment up to European standard. Even though army pay was low, the British Army cost more per soldier because it relied on volunteers.

A cost not shown is that of conscription itself. Conscription took able and productive young men out of the labor force for several years in an era when remaining life expectancy for men aged 20 was only about four decades. (And less than three decades in some of the less advanced areas.) In addition to the personal burdens this cut overall national production potential by several percent. For Germany the money cost of defense was about 3½ percent of GDP but the "blood tax" of conscription meant that the real burden was in the neighborhood of 6 percent or so. For France with her higher conscription rate it was greater yet.

The Great General Staff had, if anything tended to underrate the Russians, largely in the sense that it expected internal unrest to undermine the army's cohesion. (While it did so in the end of course, the Russian Army proved more resilient than many GGS officers had anticipated.) But in looking at the trends of growth in Russian population, GDP, military expenditure and reforms after about 1910, they grew alarmed and became convinced that Russia would soon grow into a forces as unstoppable as the tide. They began to tell themselves that it was essential to have it out with Russia now, before she became overwhelmingly powerful. Thus when a crisis arose in 1914 the GGS insisted that war was the best course.[12]

The French Army was highly rated by most experts in Europe and Britain but in fact it was a step behind Germany's in most respects, as war would prove. The German leadership, however, had no strategic intelligence service in the modern sense to weigh these factors dispassionately and sum up the implications, and the GGS (as staffs are wont to do) saw things strictly in worst-case terms; it didn't help clear thinking. Thus the seemingly hard, objective data regarding factors of strength often failed to promote clarity.[13]

The GGS had a generally more accurate assessment of its Austro-Hungarian allies and of the British and Belgian Armies. It feared that the Dual Monarchy's forces had serious weaknesses, and rightly. In fact they duplicated some of the problems of the Russians, although in attenuated form. The Habsburg state's lack of unity and cohesiveness was reflected in inability to agree on funding and support for the Army, and in some cases (although remarkably few, until the war started to go badly) resulted in units with little sense of patriotic loyalty. Moreover, the top leadership was seriously deficient.[14]

In the wake of the Boer War (when things had frequently gone badly for it) the British Army devoted a lot of effort to modernizing itself and pursuing Continental levels of effectiveness. Its troops were all long-service regulars and many of the more senior men had combat experience. But with no reserves it was small and could not immediately replace any serious losses. And it too suffered from particularly bad top leadership. The GGS had respect for the British Army but saw it as too small to exercise a decisive effect.

Belgium's army had been very small and antiquated until just before the war. The nation was neutral and not aligned with either alliance, but by 1913 her leaders decided that Germany posed a real threat in light of a series of crises and some wild statements by top German officials (including the Kaiser) as well as massive construction of rail lines up to the border, terminating in military unloading platforms. Funding was increased and a series of measures to strengthen and reform the Belgian Army embarked upon. The accomplishments by the outbreak of war remained limited however, and even with expansion the Army was small.[15]

. . .

IT WAS VERY DIFFICULT for military leaders and statesmen to understand what modern war might truly involve. The most recent wars of the major European powers were the British war against the Boer settlers in South Africa and the Russo-Japanese War in Manchuria (as the northeastern provinces of China were called). Although neither closely resembled the war that was to come in 1914, the Russo-Japanese conflict was on the whole the better predictor.

The implications of the great increases in firepower and the density of forces were only partly recognized but most cavalrymen had, with whatever reluctance, come to accept that the long era of mounted combat with the *arme blanche*—cold steel—was at last largely over, at least on European battlefields. Bodies of horsemen remained essential, it was almost universally thought, but their mission would be reconnaissance to discover the enemy's location and strength, screening to shield their own forces from enemy reconnaissance and serving as highly mobile light infantry forces.

By 1914 all European armies had embraced the machine gun and had provided themselves with various versions on a scale of one per several hundred front-line troops—virtually all of the major armies had settled on 24 machine guns per division. (Today, major armies generally have one machine gun for every handful of infantry.) The great weight of early machine guns made them very cumbersome but they were nevertheless important even in mobile warfare.[16]

But important as the machine gun unquestionably was it was overshadowed by artillery, the great executioner of both world wars. European armies had been employing artillery in the field for nearly five centuries but artillery had been revolutionized in the decade before 1905. While guns of the early 1890s had steel barrels, loaded through the breech and used smokeless powder, they still jumped back several feet with every shot and had to be manhandled into position again and re-aimed before the next one. Only a few shots could be fired by a light gun in the space of a minute, and really accurate fire was out of the question. Guns were mostly placed closely behind the lines, used as super shotguns.[17]

Figure 10. Left: German second-line reservists practice with machine gun. Right: Loading drill with French 75.

It was France that revolutionized artillery with the introduction at the end of the 1890s of the *Canon de 75 modèle 1897*, a light field gun with a 75 mm (3 in) bore. It was the first cannon with a mechanism (broadly similar in principle to the hydro-pneumatic shock absorber and spring combination of a car) for absorbing the momentum of recoil and returning the barrel smoothly to its original position while the gun carriage stayed still. Combined with a semiautomatic breech mechanism that opened and kicked out the spent shell casing as the gun recoiled, this made it possible to fire 15 well-aimed rounds per minute, each weighing 16 pounds. A practiced crew could fire at a rate of 20 rounds per minute for brief periods.

While a machine gun could spray 200 bullets into an infantry formation in 20 seconds, a French 75 could shower it with 1500 man-killing balls, using shrapnel ammunition that burst over the target area. And while the machine gun was limited to a range of a few hundred yards the 75 mm cannon could reach out to thousands of yards. Moreover, the French had devised means to aim accurately at such ranges even against targets that lay behind a hill and could not be seen from the gun.

Other armies were caught by surprise and scrambled to match the French. None had fully done so by 1914 but Germany had forged ahead in another respect. With very strong urging from the leaders of the Great General Staff, the artillery arm had developed howitzers light enough to be taken into the field. These differed from guns like the French 75 in firing a lower velocity shell at a higher angle so that it fell with a steep trajectory. This had long been understood to be very valuable in besieging fortifications, allowing the artillery to shoot over thick walls rather than try to batter through them. Moreover, the lower velocity meant lower stresses on the shell in firing, so it could have thinner walls and a stronger explosive charge.

Figure 11. German 105 mm (left) and 150 mm (right) field howitzers.

The GGS observed that field fortifications—trenches—were becoming more important and widely used as a way for infantry to escape the storm of fire on modern battlefields and reasoned that lighter and more mobile howitzers were needed to accompany mobile forces. There was substantial opposition but they prevailed and by 1914 German regular corps had both 105 mm (4.1 in) and 150 mm (5.9 in) howitzers, giving them a significant advantage in many circumstances.[*] The French and British had been late to follow, delayed by budget considerations and well as failure to recognize the utility of lighter howitzers.

(The Russians had reequipped much of their antiquated field artillery arm with howitzers, using guns purchased from German as well as French companies.[18])

---

[*] The Germans measured artillery bore diameters in centimeters, so these were designated 10.5 cm and 15 cm howitzers, but the modern standard of millimeters is used here for all artillery.

With few exceptions, however, these new-technology weapons were moved by means that had scarcely changed since the time of Napoléon or even earlier: they were drawn by teams of horses (or in very rough areas, mules), usually six to a team, eight for the heaviest guns. Horse teams were good for hauling artillery and wagons over broken ground but for traction on roads they were slow and vulnerable to injury or disease as well as demanding a great mass of fodder relative to pulling power.

Some larger guns were drawn by tractors powered by gasoline or steam engines. Many artillery officers anticipated that motor traction would replace animal teams for most large guns but limited progress had been made in that direction by 1914. The value of the truck had been recognized for ammunition supply—we'll return to that theme.

. . .

ARMIES TOOK TO THE AIR more readily than most people realize. Tethered balloons had been proving their worth for surveying the battlefield and nearby areas for well over a century. But from a balloon at 4,000 feet an observer couldn't see much more than 15 miles ahead and many officers were interested in the possibility of something to provide much wider reconnaissance. There was also some speculation about bombing from aircraft.[19]

Flying seems to hold an innate appeal to the human imagination—dreams about flying and soaring were very common long before human flight came to reality.[20] Europeans and Americans experimented both with airplanes and powered airships over the course of the 1800s and the first flyable experimental airships appeared in the 1880s.[21]

That was in France and for whatever reason it was the French who had the greatest early enthusiasm for flight. (They also took up the automobile with particular eagerness and the early German carmakers found their strongest market in Paris.[22]) The first practical airship was developed in France, flying in 1902, and the French Army bought a number of airships of modest size and performance. The German Army followed starting in 1906.[23]

For a larger airship with higher performance a rigid frame was necessary. But since airships must be lighter than air, the structure had to be extremely light for its size and strength, and correspondingly costly to build. The first practical large rigid airships were developed in Germany by Ferdinand Graf von Zeppelin, an eccentric retired general, with military uses specifically in mind. The Prussian Army was initially lukewarm at best, but soon some officers were swept up in a wave of national enthusiasm. With GGS support the War Ministry bought its first Zeppelin in 1909. But when it was found to be delicate, troublesome and temperamental in exercises the GGS soured on airships.[24]

Figure 12. Left: Zeppelin LZ 17, bombing Antwerp, September 1914.[25] Right: French troops fire at German reconnaissance plane.[26]

It turned instead to the even newer technology of airplanes, insistently calling for more planes in the years leading up to the war, feuding with the War Ministry and Inspectorate of Transport Troops which wanted to concentrate on airships. In this the Germans began well behind the French, who had been the first to embrace the military airplane, and no better than even with the British. But despite the rather chaotic direction, the Army succeeded in providing itself with a capable airplane reconnaissance force by the outbreak of war in 1914. Fighters and bombers did not come until the war was well underway.[27]

The Zeppelins proved to be just as problematic as the GGS had feared they would be.[28]

. . .

BEYOND ALL THESE NEW and powerful weapons, the Great General Staff and the more thoughtful of their foreign counterparts wrestled with the implications of the sheer scale that armies had attained. The American Civil War had involved numbers that approached those expected to fight in a European conflict, but they'd been spread over a very wide area and no one battle had involved more than about a quarter of a million men all told. In Europe there was every prospect that more than two million men would struggle over an area no larger than a single theater of the Civil War.

Figure 13. Endless columns of supply wagons.

It was not difficult to foresee that this could result in the most awful traffic-jam in human history, not to say the deadliest, made all the worse because almost everything would move at the pace of marching men and horses, trailed by endless columns of supply wagons. Whether and how vast, slow-moving, unwieldy armies could maneuver and fight in response to a coherent intent was anything but clear.

Was it possible in such circumstances to bring a war to a swift conclusion? If not, what would become of nations whose economic life depended on imports and exports? Almost a quarter of Germany's food was imported, and much of domestic agriculture depended on imported inputs. Stocks were limited and hunger threatened if a war cut off imports for more than a year. Industrial production too would be severely affected by any prolonged blockade. In particular, Germany's ability to manufacture ammunition and other vital war materials depended much on imported inputs.[29]

The mood of the GGS was both anxious and hopeful. Its leaders knew more than anyone else about the problems of maneuvering large formations. But they could see in their mind's eye how the Chief of Staff, acting in the Kaiser's name, would use the staff to collate information from reconnaissance and reports from field army commanders to form a comprehensive picture, plot out the movements and actions necessary to advance his overall concept of operations, and communicate his intentions to the army commanders using modern technology. And how the individual field army commanders would similarly guide their corps. Moreover, they had tested it all out in many maneuvers and war games over the years.

Nothing was clear or certain in war; they understood that. But they thought it could be made to work. And they believed that they could trust in the abilities and sense of their comrades who would command and direct the field armies and corps under the guidance of the doctrine that they had worked out and practiced together over years of thinking, planning, wargames, and exercises.

Figure 14. Vast, slow-moving, unwieldy armies.[30]

v. Losing the Peace

WHY COULDN'T THE STATES OF Europe live together in peace? It was one of the two richest regions in the world (the other being the European offshoot nations of North America). It was the most civilized of the world's regions (in the literal meaning of the population dwelling in cities). By all measures of wealth and human wellbeing Europe was advancing rapidly. It was hard to doubt that its states could all do best through peaceful industry and trade, and that war was unlikely to benefit even its winners by as much as peace could. Indeed, this was all laid out in a bestselling book entitled *The Great Illusion*, read by statesmen everywhere.[1]

Yet Europe had known few significant intervals of peace in the 1500 years since the decline of the Roman Empire in the West. First plunder and then territorial conquest had been the objectives of wars for European leaders over many centuries. But by the 1800s the major forms of wealth weren't portable enough to be enticing as plunder. After Germany's 1871 consolidation scarcely any room remained for expansion within Western or Central Europe without conflict with a Great Power, and Russia had already conquered all of Northeastern Europe that was worth having.

That left Southeastern Europe, the Balkan Peninsula. Outside of the region itself, few Europeans were deluded enough to see much positive value in it. It had been poor and little-civilized time out of mind, and its levels of human enlightenment and development were the lowest in Europe.[2] It was Europe's appendix, and in the decades before 1914 the continent suffered mounting appendicitis attacks.

Figure 15. The Balkans and neighboring regions.

IN A SENSE, the political and social malaise of the Balkans arose ultimately out a chill gust off the Eurasian Steppe, the great swath of grassy plains stretching from Hungary almost to the gates of Beijing, mostly too cold and dry to support forests or crops. Over millennia tribes of horse nomads streamed off the Steppe in repeated waves to raid or sometimes conquer the richer agricultural lands in Northern China, Southeastern Europe or the Middle East.

One such tribe was that of the Ottoman Turks, who settled in Anatolia (in modern-day Turkey) before 1300.[*] Like all the steppe

---

[*] Sometimes (and more accurately) called the Osmanli Turks, after Osman I (1258–1326), the leader who established their power in 1299.

horse nomads they were fierce and skilled cavalrymen, fighting from horseback with bow and sword. At that time, the southern Balkans and western Anatolia were part of the Eastern Roman Empire, centered around its capital of Constantinople.* The Roman Empire had dominated the whole Balkans and Near East for a thousand years, but it had been severely battered by other nomad groups and was much decayed by then.

In the latter 1300s the Ottomans forged across the narrow straits that link the Black Sea to the Mediterranean (later known as the Turkish Straits), invading Balkan Europe. By 1400 they controlled major portions of the Balkan and Anatolian Peninsulas, leaving only the great fortified metropolis of Constantinople itself in Byzantine hands. At last the ancient city fell to an Ottoman siege in 1453, the final act of the nearly 15-century-long drama of the Roman Empire. The Ottomans made it their capital, calling it *Kostantiniyye* (now Istanbul).

Like almost all ancient empires that of the Ottomans was built on conquest; most of its growth in wealth came from expansion of territory and population by means of the sword. When it reached the political, military, and technological limits of what it could conquer, growth slowed sharply, prompting corrosive internal struggles for shares of a largely stagnant pool of wealth.[3]

By the late 1500s the Ottomans occupied or controlled virtually the entire Balkan Peninsula, as well as most of the lands around the Black Sea. But this was near the limits at which it was possible for Ottoman armies to exert power and conquest was slowing. There was no immediate collapse, but a loss of internal cohesion and vigor started to become apparent.

. . .

WITH ITS MANPOWER resources and record of conquest the Ottoman Empire continued to loom ominously on the horizon of European Christendom, but Christian Europe was transforming itself. Drawing from the learning of the ancient Greeks and Romans, neglected for a

---

* Often called by its older Greek name of Byzantium, just as the empire was often known as the Byzantine Empire.

thousand years and more, and combining it with knowledge borrowed from the Arabs and their own discoveries, Europeans were developing a new way of understanding the world and using it to find new ways to gain wealth. They were building means to create more wealth from existing resources rather than only grabbing more resources from others, Not that they gave up conquest and exploitation of conquered resources but Europeans, particularly those in Western Europe, were inventing self-reinforcing economic growth.

As countries became richer they could afford professional, full-time armies armed with the most technologically advanced weapons and trained to execute complex tactical schemes. By the late 1600s this was coming to be the norm among the major European states.

Major states in the western and central parts of Europe, that is. Russia lagged, and the Ottomans lagged a very great deal. As the Turkish forces started losing major battles, even with superiority in numbers, attempts were made at modernization. But the forces of religious-fundamentalist conservatism were never overcome, at least not for long. There was some modernization of weapons, paid for by increasing the burdens on the peasantry, but extremely slow economic growth and no move toward army professionalization.

Hungary was not much more advanced or progressive than the Ottoman Empire that occupied much of her country, but the Habsburgs who ruled Austria had gained title to the Hungarian throne and their modern European armies pushed the Ottomans out of Hungary by the mid–1750s.[4]

Until 1700 or so most of the European elite regarded the Russians as no more European than the Turks. They were Christians to be sure, but Orthodox Christianity seemed scarcely less alien than Islam. Then came Czar Peter the Great (*Pyotr I*) (1672–1725; r. 1694–1725), who dragged, whipped, and kicked his country into Europe's orbit, ruthlessly suppressing or destroying all who opposed him. We can only speculate what might have happened if there had been a Turkish equivalent to Peter.

One of Peter's great projects was to incorporate the lands north of the Black Sea, the Ukraine, into Russia and bring them under the plow. Modernized Russian armies repeatedly defeated the Ottomans, driving them back. At the same time Russia fought Poland, then a major power whose territory included much of the Ukraine. The effort extended beyond Peter's life but Czarina Catherine the Great (*Yekaterina II*) (1729–1796; r. 1762–1796) held off the forces of internal reaction and did much to expand Russia's territory and power in Europe, and by the end of her reign the northern shores of the Black Sea were in Russia's hands. In the lands beyond grew abundant crops of grain, raised on vast estates by serf labor.

Peter's ambitions in the south had extended farther, much farther. He was determined that Russia should not only control the Black Sea and its shores but that the Turkish Straits should become the Russian Straits, under Russian control. In his plans there was no room for the Ottoman Empire in Europe or astride the Straits. Constantinople was destined to become a Russian city, he insisted.

In addition to Peter's strategic vision, there were very concrete practical reasons to seek control of the Turkish Straits. Russia was land poor; she had ample land and resources but because productivity was very low there was little liquid wealth and the government was perpetually short of money.[5] As Europe grew richer lucrative markets opened for wheat from the Ukraine—if the grain could be gotten there. Because Russia was so backward there were no railroads, even by the mid–1800s, but grain could be sent cheaply by water. The best way was to ship it from the Black Sea through the Turkish Straits into the Mediterranean Sea, either to sell it in Southern European markets or carry it on to the Atlantic for delivery to Northern Europe. But this meant that Turkish hands encircled Russia's fiscal windpipe.[6]

Peter's plan for Russian control of the Straits however did not much recommend itself to the British or French, for a strong Russian military presence in the Mediterranean would threaten their interests and security very directly. The Russians felt strongly that they had a natural "historic mission" to take over from the fading Ottomans. But industrialization was making France and Britain very rich and promoting their military power, which was changing the rules of Great-Powerdom.

Figure 16. Redrawing the Map of the Balkans, 1878–1914.[7]
(*M. marks Montenegro*)

With everyone overestimating his own strength, Britain, France and the Ottoman Empire clashed with Russia in the Crimean War (1853–1856). It left Russia with her position in the Black Sea (and Europe) seriously weakened and a recognition that it was essential to approach the Turkish Straits with cautious guile rather than blunt force.

The war also fostered enduring Russian hostility toward Austria. The Russians felt that the Austrian rulers owed them much because Russia had intervened in 1848–1849 to help Vienna crush rebels. But in the Crimean War Austria refused to support the Russians, which they saw as rank ingratitude.

At a gross level that war did little to change the map of the Balkans but the Ottomans were forced to grant internal autonomy to several provinces. All adjoined Austria-Hungary and had potential border disputes with her.

In 1877 what was on its face a good old-fashioned Christian anti-Muslim crusade boiled up, a coalition of Eastern Orthodox nations against the Ottomans, determined to right wrongs perpetrated on their co-religionists. But of course the leading Orthodox nation was Russia, which led the attack and intended to gain most.

The Western Great Powers, led by Britain, again supported the Turks in order to keep Russia in check but popular outrage at home over Turkish atrocities against Christians prevented much direct involvement. Eventually a British fleet made it emphatically clear that Russia could not occupy Constantinople. Russia imposed a harsh peace before the other Great Powers forced her to back down significantly, again emphasizing her loss of true Great Power status.

The 1878 Treaty of Berlin, ending the war, reduced Ottoman territory in the Balkans by two-thirds, setting up six sovereign states. (In practice, several of these had long been virtually independent, notably Serbia.) It also gave Austria-Hungary the right to annex Bosnia and Herzegovina in all but name—a deal St. Petersburg had made to buy Vienna's neutrality. The top frame of Figure 16 shows the effect on the map.

The tide continued to run against the Turks over the next several decades. In 1912–1913, initially with Russian encouragement, the Balkan states leagued together to attack the Ottomans, stripping them of almost all remaining European territories. Those preliminaries completed, the victors turned to fighting each other over the spoils. In the background stood St. Petersburg, which intended to use the Balkan states as proxies to gain control over the region and push the Turks into a corner.[8]

One reason that Russia was proceeding cautiously was that she had suffered her own major crash on the road to expansion. In the early 1900s she had ignored repeated strong warning signals and tried to push newly modernizing Japan aside in Manchuria and Korea. The Russian elites felt even more contempt for the Asians than for the Turks. But the Japanese, unlike the Ottomans, had not let any traditional beliefs prevent them from acquiring knowledge and using it for developing their economy and army. Russian disaster in the 1904–1905 war helped lead to a regime-threatening revolution at home and left Russia's army seriously weakened.

It was while Russia was still mending that her Foreign Minister, Count Alexander Izvolsky (1856–1918) proposed a deal with his Austro-Hungarian counterpart: if the Dual Monarchy would promise to aid Russia in gaining rights to use the Turkish Straits freely, St. Petersburg would endorse a move to formalize the Habsburg title to Bosnia-Herzegovina. Since Austria-Hungary had been occupying and administering the territories for three decades this didn't seem like so radical a step. Izvolsky's offer was duplicitous, intended to gain Russia something for nothing at the expense of her Serbian ally which was very much opposed to consolidation of the Austro-Hungarian position in Bosnia-Herzegovina.[9]

It was also ill-considered and risky. The Czar took care to hold all of the reins of power solely in his hands, keeping his ministers in the dark about what he had others of their number doing. When reaction in both Serbia and Russia to the news of the annexation proved stronger than anticipated St. Petersburg tried to lie, bluff and bluster its way out but found it could not escape without public humiliation. Since the Czar never took responsibility for any failures Izvolsky was made the scapegoat.[10]

At the end of the Napoleonic Wars, Austria had been among the greatest of Great Powers. But the social and economic challenges of the nineteenth century had not been favorable, nor met very well and by the 1900s the fragility of Austria-Hungary was becoming apparent, even as her leaders remained determined that their state would survive and continued to command considerable military resources.[11] The prudent course for Russia and Austria-Hungary's Balkan neighbors would have been to do nothing to strengthen the Habsburg monarchy's hand but to avoid pressing it to the wall while awaiting its final disintegration.

But prudence was not much valued in St. Petersburg, where Great Power status was the concern. And in Belgrade, capital of Serbia, it was held in contempt. The Serbs were the Taliban of the day, impoverished, clannish, proudly ignorant, violent and fanatic. Most were peasant smallholders living not far above subsistence. Everywhere that Serbia's rule spread was Serbianized. Those who could might pass for Serbs; otherwise the choice was to flee or be slaughtered.[12]

The chief of intelligence for the Serbian General Staff was a violent and practiced terrorist, Dragutin Dimitrijević (1876–1917), widely known as Apis, "Bull." He'd played a leading part in the 1903 regicide and coup that brought Serbia under a radical nationalist regime, and later in the brutal intimidation of non-Serbs living in the territories conquered in the 1912–13 Balkan Wars. Such credentials gave him great stature in Belgrade.

In his spare time Apis founded and directed a secret organization, "Union or Death!", more usually known as the "Black Hand." This was based on the principle that all places everywhere that had any substantial population of Serbs—or people who could by some stretch of the imagination be counted as Serbs, or compelled to become Serbs, or be "cleansed" in order to be replaced by Serbs— belonged by right under Serbian rule, that it was Serbia's holy mission to bring them the benefits of her backwardness and misgovernance regardless of what they might want and by whatever means necessary.

Bosnia-Herzegovina fit, with a substantial minority of actual Serbs as well as others who might be Serbianized with sufficient force. Thus Austria-Hungary's occupation of it in 1878 had been unnatural and the formal annexation in 1908 was a vile abomination and irremissible sin. Something had to be done, something violent of course.

In May 1914 word came of an ideal opportunity. Archduke Franz Ferdinand, the 50-year old nephew and designated heir to the Habsburg monarch, was to visit Bosnia in June with his wife. He was widely unpopular. Remarkably enough he was unpopular in Austria, Hungary, and Serbia for some of the same reasons. He had made it clear that when he succeeded his 83-year old uncle on the throne he intended to grant expanded political rights to the Slavic peoples within the Empire, transforming it virtually into an Austro-Hungarian-Slavic state, a triple monarchy. He expected this to strengthen the state and present some check to the disruptive powers of the Hungarians within it.

Figure 17. Franz Ferdinand and his wife set out on their fatal drive.

If Slavs grew more content with their place in the Empire it could undermine the Serbs' vision of uniting all southern Slavs under their domination. Thus Franz Ferdinand could not be permitted to reach the throne.

In June 1914, the Black Hand dispatched several young Bosnian hotheads (who had come to Serbia to learn terrorism from masters) to assassinate the archduke, along with his wife, during their visit to Sarajevo, Bosnia's provincial capital. Arrangements were easy because the upper ranks of the Black Hand were filled with Serbian officers and government officials, and everyone, high and low, feared to oppose it.

The amateurishness of their plot was exceeded only by the fecklessness of the security precautions for the archduke, together with his folly in visiting Bosnia at a particularly sensitive time in the first place; one of the assassins found his mark. The Austrian investigation was stumbling, but evidence pointing to Serbia and high government officials slowly accumulated.

No one in Belgrade had given much thought to the possibility that the plot would be traced to them or to the consequences if it were. As evidence of Serbian complicity was reported, the government responded with bland assurances that it was all wrong or fabricated and that Serbia was altogether innocent. It was widely known that on his own initiative the Russian minister at Belgrade had long been a strident advocate of aggressive measures against Austria-Hungary (although not the assassination specifically, so far as anyone can tell), but his government denied all responsibility and supported the Serbian denials.

In Vienna all this reinforced the arguments of those insisting that the assassinations were a part of a Russian-sponsored plan to undermine and destroy the Empire, giving Austria-Hungary no choice but to strike down Serbia, risk regardless.

At any given moment in most major capitals one may find people in high places, or waiting to occupy them at a favorable turn of governments, who see the country's enemies gathering and insist that war is essential to forestall their demonic designs, *war now*. In ordinary circumstances their violent paranoia brings them little but contempt or patronizing tolerance. But every so once in a while disturbing external events can seem to validate their warnings and spread a gloss of realism over their proposals.

Few external events are more disturbing than the assassination of a prominent government leader, even a controversial leader not particularly widely liked. Historians often seem to see the assassination of Franz Ferdinand as simply one more event, but it was an event of particular emotional impact and it upset the balance of the minds of the leadership in a way that is akin to, for instance, that of the September 11, 2001 terrorist attacks in the United States. Seemingly rational arguments that it somehow "should" not have had so much impact are vacuous denials of the essential nature of our minds.

Certainly Vienna had long had its "hawks" who called for war on Serbia (and/or Italy, Russia, or various others). Franz Ferdinand was no paragon of prudent and moderate public leadership but he had striven to dampen their influence and his assassination was well calculated to set the dogs loose.

There was in any event no real Austro-Hungarian interest in expansion into the Balkans beyond Bosnia-Herzegovina. The leaders much preferred the Balkans "Balkanized" with weak, non-threatening states and swore that there would be no annexation of any Serbian territory at all.[13]

What truly was the intent of the assassination? The intent not of the teenage gunmen but of the men in Belgrade who indoctrinated, armed, prepared and sent them on their way? It seems very possible that it was to set in motion just what it did, a war that would open the way for a South-Slav state—Yugoslavia—that Serbs could dominate. Ironically Bosnia ultimately became one of the great victims of Serbian nationalism, eight decades later.

But whatever the intent, the assassination of the heir to the thrones of Austria and Hungary made it much harder to resist calls to arms. Still important figures held back, seeking alternatives or reassurance. Germany was the most prominent place to look for both and a top-level emissary was dispatched—Alexander Graf von Hoyos (1876–1937), chief of staff to the Austro-Hungarian foreign minister—bearing a message from the aged Habsburg Emperor to the Kaiser and a memorandum explaining the necessity for war.

In Kaiser Wilhelm II's book no crime was blacker than regicide, nor more deserving of condign punishment. He drew Austria-Hungary a "blank cheque," a promise of German backing against Russia if it came to that. Surely it would never have to be honored, he imagined, for his younger cousin Czar Nicholas II (*Nicolay II*) (1868–1918; r. 1894–1917) would never allow his country to go to war in defense of regicides. Top officials who ought to have had clearer minds willingly countersigned.

The Kaiser did not in any real sense control or direct German policy, but the cumulative influence of his wooly and erratic blustering had over the years exerted a corrosive effect. While he might not be right he could never be wrong, not in public at least, nor to his face, and that severely restricted any possibility of arguing against the dark imaginings of those who warned that Germany was being encircled by malign forces. While the events in Sarajevo did not spread alarm in Berlin—it wasn't *their* prince, after all—with Germany supposedly facing enemies on all sides it was essential to stand with her only ally of any consequence, Austria-Hungary.

That said, however, for most of Germany's leaders it was really rather abstract. Some of the top officers of the Army aside, there was little support for any immediate measures even to increase military readiness.

The assurance of German support did not lead to an immediate consensus in Vienna, but ultimately it was agreed that Serbia had to be rendered incapable of exercising her evil designs. (It was accepted, despite some insistence to the contrary, that it would never work to try to conquer Serbia and incorporate the Serbs into the Austro-Hungarian Empire.) Finally, almost four weeks after the assassinations, demands were presented to Belgrade. They were deliberately harsh; Vienna had little interest in compromise. While sweetly worded, Serbia's reply offered few concessions of substance. And it was accompanied by orders to mobilize the Serbian Army.

The Russians were determined to prevent Austria-Hungary from defeating Serbia. This was essential for their Balkans and Turkish Straits ambitions, but beyond that they saw it as crucial to their Great Power status. Russia's standing had never really recovered from the Crimean War debacle, and the Czar and his circle believed that was why the other Great Powers had ganged up to thwart Russia repeatedly in the past. With real economic strength finally on the horizon they felt an urgency to push back, even at the risk of war. That it would have been far better and safer to wait until the promised economic strength was actually in hand does not appear to have weighed much in their calculations.

It seems possible that the Serbs might have back-pedaled vigorously enough to deprive Vienna of sufficient excuse for war if the Russians had warned them sharply, but St. Petersburg never jerked their leash, no more than Berlin jerked Austria-Hungary's.[14] The French had some reason for interest in preventing the destruction of Serbia, for they had lent her a great deal of money.[15] Their real concern, however, was mutual solidarity with Russia. The French President at the time was Raymond Poincaré (1860–1934), a prominent Germanophobe who believed strongly that if France and Russia stood firmly behind Serbia then Austria-Hungary and Germany would blink. And if there was to be war with Germany then let it be now, when Russia felt her own vital interests were at risk and was thus sure to lend her full strength to the fight. So Poincaré wrote St. Petersburg a blank cheque to match the Kaiser's for Vienna.

If the pressures caused the breakup of the Dual Monarchy then so much the better from the standpoint of both Russia and France. That would leave Germany without allies and thus less able to threaten either. And Russia would stand to pick up some choice Slavic provinces, either as parts of the Empire or satellite states.

Berlin gave Russia very clear warning that preparations for war in the west would mean swift attack, regardless of whether she had formally declared war or even announced full mobilization. St. Petersburg indignantly denied any intent to make war against Germany but quietly built up nevertheless.

Austria-Hungary announced mobilization, strictly against Serbia and without actually calling troops up. Russia ordered mobilization against her but worries that partial mobilization would interfere with readiness to fight Germany led to full mobilization on the following day. No diplomatic announcement was made but since mobilization could not be concealed from German diplomats and agents in the country, silence only made it seem more pointed toward aggression. Germany warned that continuation would mean war, and then mobilized and declared war when Russia failed to respond. France ordered full mobilization before receiving news of German mobilization. Germany presented an ultimatum to Belgium—open the frontiers to German troops and allow them free transit or be invaded.

. . .

BRITAIN HELD BACK BRIEFLY. The Entente with France and later with Russia had been the work of a small circle of men centered after 1905 about the Foreign Secretary, Sir Edward Grey (1862–1933).[*] For most Britons, Grey definitely included, imperial and colonial issues strongly colored attitudes toward the European Powers. Britain had struck a fairly stable colonial compromise with France and Grey worked out a limited one with Russia but he was concerned about what he perceived as the hostile attitude of the Germans.[16]

Grey hoped and worked for a negotiated settlement. It was the position of his Liberal Party and his own personal inclination. He issued several calls for a multinational summit conference, but scarcely any of the Continental states really supported him. We know that the proposals had no effect and there is a tendency to view them as naïvely ineffectual or even insincere, but this isn't realistic. Grey had achieved some success along these lines in previous crises and it wasn't obvious that this time was so different.

Like the vast majority of Britons, Grey had not accepted that he was a European and that Britain was a European country. He was a four-square English country gent, "high-minded, simple, kindly, and wise,"[17] devoted to a wife comfortable nowhere but at their country estate. Although intelligent, Grey had no intellectual distinction or interests. His own concerns about issues of foreign policy were Imperial, not European, at least until the last years before the war. He

---

[*]   Grey was a baronet, a hereditary title quite closely equivalent to the German "von."

visited colonies but never Europe until the eve of war. He knew a little French but felt easy speaking no language other than English.

Figure 18. Sir Edward Grey in 1914.

So Grey largely lacked the sort of diplomatic capital that Bismarck had built so assiduously and invested so effectively. He had no deep relationships with any of the major European leaders and hadn't even met those who had spent no time in England. He couldn't say to any of them, "Do this for me, for our friendship; I beg you." Moreover he was late. Although Britain had once been a pioneer in strategic intelligence, she was far behind the Continental Great Powers in this in 1914, with the result that neither Grey nor anyone else in the Cabinet was aware that something terribly dangerous was brewing until Vienna presented its ultimatum to Serbia on July 23. By that point such opportunities for effective mediation as there may have been had largely passed by. None of Grey's proposals for a settlement short of war ever was answered by much positive response.[18]

By the last days of July it was apparent that the avalanche could not be stopped, that in Grey's haunting phrase, the lights were going out one by one. Grey felt that Britain could not step aside, that she must stand with France. We cannot know exactly why; Grey himself may not have known the whole of it. But he feared German ambition and aggression, and the prospect of Belgium and France under German domination definitely seemed distinctly fearsome.

The decision in Britain rested with the Cabinet, although it had to take very serious account of the support it could expect from Parliament and ultimately the people. The ruling Liberal Party had historically been against war and European ties. It had been struggling to regain and maintain a coherent political identity and many of its leaders feared that to take Britain into a European war could mean the end for it—as it practically did. Unsurprisingly only a minority of the Cabinet (and Party) stood with Grey in favor of Continental intervention while neither of the Liberals' coalition allies, the Irish Nationalists or Labour, had any enthusiasm at all. The question was debated intensely over several meetings, with only a little movement in Grey's direction.[19]

Grey's strongest points centered in various ways on Belgium. There was for one thing a question of law, European order, and British honor. Britain, along with all the other powers, had guaranteed the independence and neutrality of Belgium in a treaty of 1839. If Europe was not to become a perpetual battleground, Grey insisted, its smaller states needed to have some protection from larger predators, and the Belgian treaty was a prominent test of this. It would be both deeply dishonorable and profoundly subversive of European order for Britain to abandon Belgium in the face of invasion.[20]

Such arguments of principle appealed to Grey and to his Liberal colleagues although many were less ready than he to embrace them. But Grey also raised a much starker argument of power politics. If Germany conquered and made satellites of Belgium and France, he proposed, then the Netherlands, surrounded by German-dominated territory, could scarcely resist her demands. No more could Denmark. This would put all of the Atlantic coasts of Europe from the Baltic entrance to the Pyrenees under the control of a demanding and ambitious power possessed of great wealth, free to resume her naval buildup. In such circumstances, Grey warned, Britain could scarcely avoid falling under German domination herself.

Behind all this, not elaborated but widely understood, was the sense that Britain needed to live in a neighborhood with order and regularity, a society of states which accepted and lived by certain moderating rules of behavior, a just and moral order. Like the British Constitution the order was understood implicitly and subject to a certain flexibility of interpretation. But like the Constitution this did not make it any less real or important in British eyes.

More than a century earlier, alarm that the French revolutionaries and then Napoléon were kicking over the established European order had drawn Britain into the greatest and most intense struggle in European history up to the twentieth century. In fact of course Britain had been contesting with France for European dominance at intervals since the fourteenth century and the Hundred Years War. But in national memory the conflict with the revolutionaries and particularly the "bloody tyrant" Napoléon was special, a war of high principle. In British eyes its purpose had been to establish not merely British supremacy but the just and moral order in Europe. They felt deeply committed to this order, much as Americans feel committed to the post-World War II/Cold War order.

Many Germans recognized the British attitude toward the post-Napoleonic settlement in Europe, and many who did resented it bitterly. The British idealization of the European order appeared to them to be a cynical and corrupt justification for a system that worked to British advantage, against Germany's interests.

Belgium was pivotal. Her neutrality had been guaranteed by Britain, Austria, France, Germany and the Netherlands, and to the British was an integral element of the European order. For German armies to cut through a minor and little-populated corner of Belgium in the south might not upset the whole order, but invasion and subjugation of the nation surely would. Some in the German leadership did not understand this clearly, while others did but did not accept it.

Even as concern about German intentions mounted in London in the first two days of August however, the majority of the Cabinet remained skeptical and a substantial minority were strongly committed to formally declaring Britain's neutrality. Only a handful stood with Grey for supporting France. The best he could achieve was authorization to request both France and Germany to guarantee that they would respect Belgian neutrality, as long as the other did. He knew that France would give him what he wanted; the object was to put Germany on the spot. The Germans replied that they could not answer without revealing their war plans, making a German invasion of Belgium all but certain. Still the Cabinet hesitated.[21]

On August 2, after Russia, Germany, and France had all announced mobilization and Germany had declared war on Russia, the pressure on the Cabinet mounted. If it could not agree on so crucial an issue it would dissolve, and the result would almost inevitably be a change of governments, installing conservatives who had already made clear their determination to go to war. Finally on August 2 (after learning that Germany had violated the neutrality of Luxemburg) the Cabinet agreed that Britain must intervene if Germany violated Belgian neutrality in a truly major way.

Two days later Germany did precisely that. When she spurned a demand to withdraw from Belgian territory, Britain went to war with widespread support in Parliament and the public.[22]

. . .

THE FIRST WORLD WAR redrew the map of Europe and the world as a whole, but it wasn't fought for territory, not initially. Later, to be sure, some states joined with one side or the other in return for promises of lands—Italy, Bulgaria, Romania and even distant Japan were the notable ones—and as the war ground on most combatants came to demand territory in compensation. But other than perhaps Serbia none of the original participants had any definite territorial agenda.

This seems wrong to many people, who "know" that the Germans engineered the whole thing because they wanted to—well, they wanted to conquer somewhere or other. Naturally there truly were people in Germany who did dream of conquering one place or another, just as there were in all of the major countries. But they had no political power, especially not in Germany whose leaders could see no attractive targets for additions to the Reich.

In the course of the war German leaders expressed territorial ambitions just as leaders of all the major combatants did (other than the United States, which joined the fight in 1917). In the case of Germany (but not that of others), prominent historians have insisted that the leaders "must have" held these objectives before the war, but they can produce no documentary evidence.[23] The documents all point to absence of German pre-war territorial ambitions.[24] Germany's leaders wanted no more ethnic dilution, and aside from Austria there were no predominantly German-speaking areas beyond the Empire. Nor were there any territories of special strategic or economic value.[25]

What Germany wanted was what all the major participants wanted, in various forms: security and power. In Germany's case it was not so much the power to achieve specific ends, like Russia's insistence on the power to exercise effective control over the Balkans and the Turkish Straits, as the nebulous, all-encompassing power to assure her greatness, her superiority. Her power ambitions didn't definitely and directly intrude on anyone else's in any specific way but they made everyone feel very crowded.

That wouldn't have brought war in itself, to be sure. But with Austria-Hungary threatening a key Russian client the determination that her power (such as it was) needed to be preserved to assure Germany's defense clashed directly with St. Petersburg's most dearly-held power ambitions, ambitions regarded as essential to preservation of Russia's Great Power status.

France could well have said that Russia's Balkan ambitions were no concern of hers and in fact had done so earlier in the 1908 Bosnian crisis. But Germany's erratic blustering pursuit of power had left Paris convinced that security could only be guaranteed through tight mutual defense ties with a powerful Russia. The resulting pledge of all-out French military support emboldened Russia to support the Serbs, emboldening the Serbs in turn to defy Austria-Hungary. But by the same token Germany's pledge of unlimited support emboldened Vienna to challenge Belgrade.

Viewed in this light, the whole web of causation all seems too in-substantial to have supported so desperate and costly a struggle. Why could it not have been possible to negotiate a settlement that would have been reasonably satisfactory to all the major states? It might well have been, with Britain as the logical go-between. She had links to France and Russia but no formal ties or overriding shared interests, and her relations with Germany had been taking a generally positive turn.*

But in essence Berlin and Vienna had ambushed Britain and any peace efforts she might mount by conspiring to maintain an outward appearance of relative tranquility until the ultimatum was presented to Serbia on July 23. Russia was able to penetrate the veil of secrecy a week or so in advance but she had no more interest in British media-tion than did Germany. In the end Britain was left with the choice of joining France and Russia or attempting to remain neutral.

On July 28 the Kaiser thought better of his blank cheque for Vi-enna and tried to close the account. The German Chancellor, Theo-bald von Bethmann Hollweg, complied only perfunctorily. By the small hours of July 30 however Bethmann had grown much more concerned about what Germany had helped to set in motion and urged the Dual Monarchy to negotiate intensively and proceed cir-cumspectly.[26]

But it was far too late; Europe's funeral pyre had already been lit and could not be extinguished or contained.

---

* Starting in 1912 Germany had throttled back on the naval race.

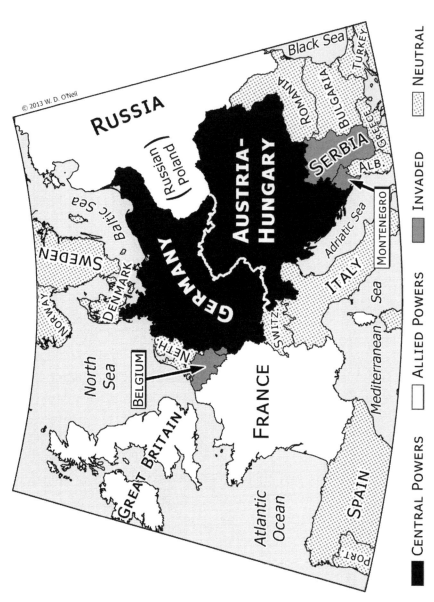

Figure 19. Europe, August 1914.

VI. The Cruelest Month

Author's Note

This chapter traces the military actions of the first weeks of the war. This is done in order to establish certain points that I need for the main arguments made later in the book. If you're interested in military history, or simply want to understand what I am saying as deeply as possible, you'll want to read it. If not however, you may safely jump to the final Chapter Summary on page 89. As long as you're prepared to take my word regarding the military action this will tell you all you need to know to comprehend the rest of the book well.

THE WAR'S CRUELEST MONTH WAS August of 1914, when men died faster than in any other. But scarcely anyone foresaw that before the conflict was joined.

It was best not to be identified as the aggressor, responsible for starting the war; everyone understood that. (Russia and France later altered their diplomatic records to obscure Russia's responsibility.) The Germans in particular held off their mobilization for several days, even as the military leaders warned with mounting stridency that the Russians, with their head start, might attack before Germany could be ready to defend herself. Finally, the step was taken on the afternoon of August 1.[1]

France's leaders too had been in a frenzy of apprehension, goaded by their own generals, fearful of being caught flat-footed, before at last they agreed to mobilize. This came less than an hour before the decision in Berlin. In fact leaders in both capitals decided on mobilization before knowing the decision of the others; in practical effect the decisions were simultaneous.

The German Army (really the various German state armies that constituted it) needed 13 days to mobilize all its men, complete their outfits of clothing, equipment and weapons, muster them into units and transport them to their concentration areas. French intelligence had given reasonably good information on how long it took. Similarly the German Great General Staff understood that France, with her compact geography and good rail net, would be a day or two quicker in mobilizing. Russia's vast territory and limited railroads slowed mobilization considerably—but she had gotten a head start through early mobilization and earlier preparations.

Of course operations could be launched at any time with whatever forces were already available. Yet aside from minor incidents resulting from accident or local overeagerness there were no attacks across the borders separating the major combatants until August 7 when as they had agreed, Russia and France both invaded Germany. French forces thrust from Belfort into Alsace, one of the provinces annexed by Germany in 1871, taking the city of Mulhouse without significant opposition. (See Figure 20 for the location.) This was no very serious threat to the Germans, who quickly and effectively counterattacked with the weakest of the seven field armies they had deployed along their western border.

Also on the 7th two Russian armies invaded East Prussia, the long tongue of German land that lapped out along the Baltic coast. (See Figure 19 for its location.) German forces in that region were deliberately weak for reasons we'll explore later, and as a result the Russian attack caused some anxious times.

By then the Germans had already launched a major offensive in the west, not into France (not directly) but Belgium.

Belgium was neutral, a status imposed and guaranteed by an 1839 multinational treaty to which Germany was a prominent party.

Brussels had played strictly by the rules, endangering no one, supporting no one. But Germany's "military necessity" demanded that her troops march through Belgium to strike at Northern France; so the GGS had determined. The GGS master plan, widely if somewhat misleadingly known as the "Schlieffen Plan," was to knock France out of the war at least for a time with a decisive initial attack, so that Germany's armies could be free to move east to deal with Russia. The tissue of Belgium's neutrality could not be allowed to interfere.

The German war plans had been formulated by the GGS under the direction of *Generaloberst* (four-star general) Helmuth von Moltke the Younger (1848–1916), nephew of the Moltke who had led the GGS and German Army to victory in the Wars of Unification. The nephew's plans allocated the bulk of forces to the Western Front with only a single field army of just 4½ maneuver corps to defend against the Russians. Figure 20 shows the initial alignment of German and French forces in the West (also the Belgian Army, as well as the British forces once they got there). Each outline traces the concentration area for one field army, from a little over 100,000 to more than 300,000 men. The farther to the right along the German line the larger the army size, so that the right wing opposite the Belgian border much outweighed the left ranged against France proper.

The French and Germans mobilized equivalent numbers of reservists in 1914 but from Figure 20 it seems as if the German frontline forces must have been larger—as they were.

In both armies the youngest, most recently released reservists filled vacancies in active-duty units, raising them to full wartime strength. Both armies also had whole reserve units that in peacetime were skeletons with small cadres of officers and NCOs but were filled out with older reservists upon mobilization. These units weren't as ready or fully armed as their regular counterparts and the French (after acrimonious internal debate) had decided to keep theirs out of the front line.

The Germans did however put many reserve units and formations up front—even many whole corps. Some of them paid a price for their lower readiness, limited artillery, and lack of reconnaissance airplanes but on the whole the German reserve formations were effective and made a great contribution. In fact the average German reserve unit was probably at least a match for French regular units of equivalent size and the average German regular unit was significantly better.[2] It took the French command several weeks of accumulating intelligence information to recognize that they were fighting forces augmented with large numbers of reserve formations of good fighting quality.

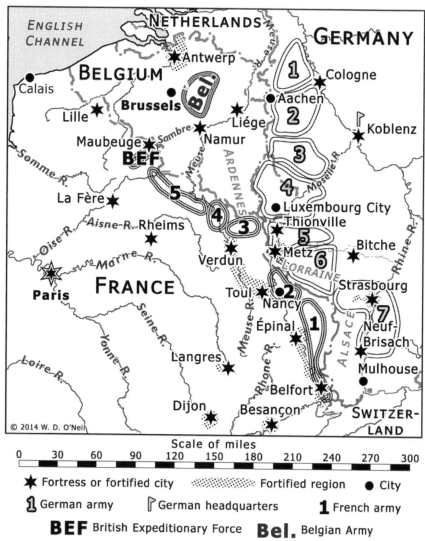

Figure 20. Initial deployments.

(A note on terminology: A military *unit* generally consists of troops all drawn from one branch or arm—infantry, artillery, cavalry, etc. A *formation* usually combines units from two or more arms integrated under one commander. In the German Army divisions, corps and field armies were all formations in this sense.)

From a military standpoint, the French would have done well to emphasize defense rather than offense at least initially. The country presents many substantial natural obstacles to an invader, particularly to the east, and these had been reinforced at critical points by the world's strongest and most extensive system of fortifications.[3] Even though the French forces had fewer front-line troops and lower effectiveness it's reasonable to expect that by making intelligent use of the terrain and fortresses they could have held off any invading Germans and inflicted heavy casualties while losing little territory. Their commanders insisted on launching offensives at the outset of the war and came close to losing it as a result.

For a number of years after the defeats of 1870 French plans did center on defense. But sentiment began to shift around the turn of the century and the generals soon committed to an offensive strategy, urged on by political leaders. In essence they saw the offense as essential to military and national morale and convinced themselves that the high morale it engendered would be a key element in enabling the offense to prevail. They sought to win any war with Germany, not just avoid losing it, and for this an offensive strategy was essential. Tragically for France, it wasn't a prudent calculation.[4]

In a nation with a long history of monarchist military *coups d'état* political leaders were understandably wary of the army. In 1911 they found a commander they felt confidence in, *Général* Joseph Joffre (1852–1931). The son of a barrel maker, and barrel-shaped himself, Joffre was a military engineer whose service had largely been in the colonies. He had no notable qualifications as a strategist or military commander—certainly nothing like the preparation of his German opponent-to-be—but had a great deal of experience in working with the political leadership. They credited him with secular, republican sympathies that recommended him strongly to the secular, republican government that appointed him.[5]

Just a few months after Joffre's appointment Poincaré became President of France. He was suspicious and fearful of Germany and believed that France's security depended on her alliance with Russia and that the Russian link depended wholly on a mutual commitment to launch offensives at the earliest possible moment in a war so as to prevent the Germans from defeating first one and then the other. Thus he strongly backed Joffre's inclination toward an offensive strategy.

. . .

LIÈGE* IN NORTHEASTERN BELGIUM was crucial to the German plans because so many main roads and rail lines toward Northern France ran through it. Moltke's plan depended on Germany's most powerful forces sweeping through Belgium and Northern France around the end of the French line. Entering Belgium further south would put the Germans in the rough country of the Ardennes plateau where unfavorable terrain and sparse rail and road routes would slow the advance, and also keep them on the wrong side of the Meuse River. Using the Liège gateway the armies could advance to the west of the Meuse on the coastal plain right to the gates of Paris with the fewest possible obstacles. This can be seen in Figure 21, a schematic diagram depicting the terrain and underlying geologic structures of the region.

Liège had been fortified for a thousand years. By the early 1800s there was a walled citadel on the heights, as well as bastions at other critical points near the town.[6] If manned by a strong garrison, these could make capturing Liège a lengthy and costly task in that era.

After Belgium was established as an independent and neutral state in 1839 not much attention had been paid to defenses. But when France and Germany went to war in 1870s Belgians grew anxious that one or the other might cross their territory to gain a tactical advantage, drawing them unwillingly into the war. Although this didn't come about, the memory prompted moves to strengthen Belgium's defenses after the war.

---

*   Lüttich in German. It was then often spelled Liége.

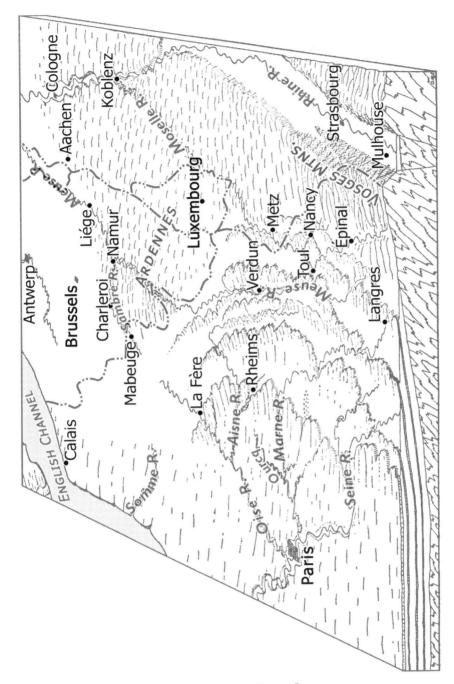

Figure 21. Landforms.[7]

The existing fortifications of Liège and other Belgian strategic points could offer no protection against the new long-range smokeless-powder cannon firing high-explosive shells. After much debate it was decided to build very costly new-style fortifications for Liège and Namur—another rail hub two days' march to the southwest—as well as the port city of Antwerp which housed the Belgian Army's headquarters and main base. Figure 20 shows numerous towns and cities marked by fortress symbols, many of which the German armies could bypass. But Liège and Namur had to be taken, and without delay.

The towns were surrounded by rings of subterranean forts four to six miles out from the city center, each capped with a shield of concrete as thick as 13 feet, with only low, rounded, armored gun turrets and observation posts standing proud of the surface. (See Figure 25.) They were designed to withstand fire from 210mm (8.25in) guns, the heaviest then in use, and those of Liège and Namur were intended to stand off an attack for 30 days in order to give the Belgian Army the time it needed to mobilize.[8]

For the GGS, a thirty-day delay would be a disaster, eclipsing any hope of dealing with the French and Russian threats separately. The fortifications around Liège had to be neutralized in less than two weeks and those of Namur not long after.

Figure 22. Meuse River bridge at Liège, blown by the Belgians.

Moltke and his staff hoped that the Belgians simply would not resist the mighty army invading their lands, but they understood that they could not count on this, so they laid plans to overcome resistance quickly. Crack brigades were kept fully-manned and ready, even in peacetime, prepared to storm the forts as soon as war broke out. As long as no warning was given, the GGS calculated, the Belgians would have no time to man and prepare the forts for war so resistance would be minimal.[9]

Nothing went according to plan.

Seeing the wave of conflict rolling in their direction the Belgians mobilized effective August 1 and immediately started putting the Liège forts in readiness. The German ultimatum (presented in German at 7P.M. on August 2 with a 12-hour deadline) was greeted with defiance and the bridges across the Meuse River were destroyed, impeding initial German operations. The attempt to storm the fortifications on the night of August 5/6 went badly with heavy losses and meager gains: the town of Liège was captured but it was of little value so long as the outer forts continued to fight.[10]

The German Second Army, which was responsible for clearing the way, brought up its heavy artillery, 210mm howitzers. They were massive, unwieldy weapons weighing seven tons that had to be broken down in two loads for towing and reassembled before firing. Their 250lb shells could reach as far as $5\frac{1}{3}$ miles and were very effective against ordinary fortifications. But although they had been designed a quarter of a century earlier when weapons were less powerful the Liège forts proved able to stay in action even after 4,000 direct hits. Under a continuing firefall with shells landing every few seconds, two forts were knocked out in six days. But that was only one-sixth of the Liège forts and at that rate it would be mid-September before the route to Northern France could be opened.

Figure 23. German 210 mm howitzer.

BUT THE GGS HAD a secret weapon, ready only just barely in time—a howitzer not of 210 mm bore diameter but 420 mm (16.5 in), hurling 1,800 lb shells. It was intended to aid the Army in battering its way through the array of powerful, modern forts that France was building to guard her frontier with Germany.[11]

With the very strong urging of Schlieffen and then Moltke, Krupp had built first a 305 mm (12in) and then a 420 mm howitzer. But these were truly massive weapons that had to be transported by a special railway train to a site where a timber and steel foundation had been prepared and then erected in place. The 420 mm version weighed 150 tons and occupied ten railway cars.

Figure 24. M-Gerät ready for movement.

The GGS loved the performance of this beast but was appalled by its immobility. It insisted on a weapon of similar capability that could be moved by road and would not require a time-consuming foundation to be laid. It was a tremendous challenge, but in just two years Krupp developed a 420 mm howitzer mounted on a huge wheeled carriage and weighing 42 tons. It was broken down into five assemblies for travel on the roads, dragged at a brisk walking pace by a heavy tractor, with the 120-man gun crew marching behind.

Two of these, deceptively code-named *M-Gerät* (M-apparatus) or *Kurze Marinekanone* (short naval cannon) for secrecy, were completed and tested by mid–1914 and rushed to Liège, coming into action on August 12. The low, broad forts, built before steel reinforcement for concrete, were ideal targets and the huge guns contributed greatly to speeding their defeat. By the morning of August 16, just four days after they started firing in earnest, the last of the forts had been destroyed or put out of action.

Columns of German troops began at once to pour through Liège on the road to France. The siege guns, now augmented by Škoda 305 mm weapons lent (with crews) by Austria-Hungary, moved on down the road to Namur.[12]

Figure 25. A Liège fort destroyed by bombardment.

The Belgians were the richest people in Europe, but suffered deep ethnic and political divisions which led to neglect of defense among other problems. It was only in the last two years before the war that Belgium instituted real conscription and made a little beginning on modernizing her army. By 1918 she would have had a fairly substantial force but in 1914 the Belgian Army was still small, ill-trained and antiquated. Raw courage was not enough.

Divisions were detached to defend Liège and Namur while the balance of the army deployed behind them in Central Belgium with the hope that the German advance could be delayed until French help arrived. But Joffre was concentrating on assaults against the Germans in Alsace-Lorraine and the Ardennes, not responding to the invasion of Belgium and all the bravery of Belgium's army could do little to slow the far bigger and more capable forces of the German Second Army.

The French asked that the Belgian Army march south to link with their forces but instead it was pulled back north to its base at Antwerp where it could occupy fortified positions. In so doing the

Belgians tied down two German first-line corps plus miscellaneous second-line formations for the next several weeks, which was probably as great a contribution as their limited strength could realistically make.[13] And the stalwart defense of Liège certainly cost the Germans some grief, although whether it delayed their advance and if so exactly by how long and with what consequence is disputed.

**Figure 26. Left: Krupp 420 mm M-Gerät siege howitzer.
Right: Škoda 305 mm siege mortar.**[*]

The fortifications were captured just in time for the First Army to march through as soon as it had been fully mobilized and so in that sense the defense imposed no delay at all. But the Second Army troops that were besieging Liège could have done much mischief elsewhere if not kept so occupied. It's not accurate to claim, as the German commanders did, that Liège had no effect on the advance, but it's not really possible to express the effect in terms of a specific number of days of delay.[14] One possibility is that if Liège had fallen quickly the Second Army would have been able to prevent the Belgian Army from gaining shelter behind Antwerp's fortifications, thus freeing the two corps that had to be left behind at Antwerp.

As mentioned on page 68, on August 7—while Moltke's forces were battering their way into Northern Belgium—Joffre launched a portion of his against the German frontier to the extreme southeast,

---

[*]   These had been built to attack the border forts of Italy, then an Austro-Hungarian ally, at least on paper. As Italy did not enter the war until May 1915 the Dual Monarchy had no need of the weapons in 1914.

VI. The Cruelest Month 79

close to the Swiss border. The French forces here enjoyed some numerical edge but faced unfavorable terrain and qualitatively superior German forces. Effective counterattacks soon inflicted serious losses and forced the attackers back to the protection of the defensive belts near Belfort .

In reality this initial French attack was more a gesture than a serious offensive since only a fraction of Joffre's forces were involved and it was obvious that this was not a sector of strategic importance to Germany. For the time being Frances's Russian allies were left to do the real work. In this they obliged, advancing at the same time with two partly-mobilized field armies into East Prussia, opposed by only a single German field army.

As seen in Figure 20, Joffre had five armies in the field and he could also call on the BEF. While the Germans in Belgium were completing the reduction of the Liège fortifications the rightmost two French armies began an advance into Lorraine between Strasburg and Metz together with a smaller renewed thrust further south in the direction of Mulhouse. The Germans had always expected offensives in these areas and Moltke wanted to give ground in Lorraine to draw the French armies into a sack where they could be encircled and annihilated. But the French were too cautious and after a few days the German commander on the left demanded to be freed to counterattack. The French were forced to retreat with substantial losses but there was no envelopment or annihilation.

It was evident to French intelligence that the German forces in Lorraine were strong and that Liège was being assaulted by a substantial force. Still unaware that the German front-line forces included capable major reserve formations, they concluded that the enemy center must be lightly held. It was there that Joffre decided to direct his heaviest blow, launching the Third and Fourth Armies northeast through Luxemburg, passing north of Thionville in the direction of Koblenz. (See Figure 20 for the geographic relationships.) This would take them through the rugged and heavily wooded Ardennes region.[15]

To guard the left flank of the advance Joffre ordered the Fifth Army to march rapidly north along the west (left) bank of the Meuse

River to the area southwest of Namur. The newly-arrived British Expeditionary Force (BEF) would join them there.

The Ardennes offensive made good strategic sense. Schlieffen
had studied such a response and warned that it could pose a serious
danger of isolating the right wing, opening it to defeat in detail. But
no good came of it for the French. To the surprise of commanders on
both sides the two French armies met the German Fourth and Fifth
armies coming the other way on August 22. The German forces had
fewer troops and artillery than the French but they were more numerous than Joffre had counted on. Worse still they were substantially better in training, command and tactical preparation. The
French lost heavily, forced back on the great fortress of Verdun.[16]

**Figure 27. Incompatibles: BEF commander Sir John French (left)
and French Fifth Army commander Charles Lanrezac (right).**

Before this Joffre had been urging his Fifth Army commander,
Général Charles Lanrezac (1852–1925), to be more aggressive. But
Lanrezac held back behind the Sambre and Meuse Rivers. Reports
from the Belgians and his own reconnaissance suggested that the
German strength before him was much greater than Joffre had as-
sessed. Lanrezac was reluctant to push on northeastward as Joffre
wished without a clearer and more reassuring picture of what lay
ahead. The Sambre Valley was too narrow, shallow and crowded with

industry to make a strong defensive line but the rising and hilly ground to the south of it was generally defense-friendly. To the east, excellent defensive positions could be found along the bluffs commanding the deep, steep-sided valley of the Meuse River.

The BEF was small and not overly capable but it rejoiced in a grandly-titled commander, Field Marshall Sir John French (1852–1925).[17] Ironically, French spoke little French and got on quite badly with his eponymous allies; he and Lanrezac came to loathe one another virtually on sight. Naturally the BEF and the Fifth Army never cooperated closely, imperiling both. To ease confusion, we'll refer to the BEF commander as "Sir John" rather than "French."

The BEF had initially stood south of the Sambre between the Fifth Army on its right and extending beyond the fortress of Maubeuge on its left (as seen in Figure 20). There it had guarded the left flank of the French-British line stretching from Maubeuge to Belfort, 225 miles to the southeast, occupying a reasonably defensible position not directly exposed to the German axis of advance. Since only light screening forces stood in the path of an enemy further west this was a prudent disposition of Sir John's meager forces.

On the evening of the 20th however, he issued orders to the BEF to march north, acting in response to the urgings of Joffre, who was not well informed about the situation in Belgium, and without consulting Lanrezac. Reconnaissance was spotty and limited and no provision was made for advance guards. By nightfall on the 21st the leading forces had reached the village of Mons and the narrow industrial canal that ran through it, east to west. This was approximately six miles or half a day's march north of Lanrezac's front lines and there was a gap of more than that between the right of the BEF's lines and the left of Fifth Army's, bridged only by a thinly-stretched screen of cavalry.[18]

Unknowingly, the Fifth Army and BEF lay in the path of three German armies whose total strength greatly outweighed theirs. The First Army formed the very right of the German line and thus came opposite the BEF, on the left of the Allied line. The Second Army, next in line, opposed Lanrezac's Fifth Army. Then, separated by the Belgian fortress of Namur (which would hold out until August 24), came the German Third Army. According to later German calculations, a total of 358 German battalions with 2,164 guns were to face 257 French and British battalions with 1,120 guns; in infantry the Germans had a numerical edge of 7:5, in artillery nearly 2:1.[19] To add to the Allied disadvantage the German forces were quite distinctly better in their tactical capabilities, battalion for battalion. It was a David and Goliath contest in which it was the giant who had the stronger weapons and greater skill at arms.

A few hours before Sir John ordered his two corps north Moltke issued orders to the three right-wing German armies. He wanted the 21st to be spent getting all the forces up on the line so they could launch a massive, coordinated attack on the following day. Second Army would then push its way south across the Sambre to hit Lanrezac's army in its front and keep it pinned in place while the German First Army wrapped around its left flank and the Third Army surged across the Meuse to take the French on their right flank. There was no provision for attacking the BEF—the Supreme Army HQ intelligence did not think it was yet in place. As soon as possible the Namur forts were to be attacked as well. It was a classic plan in the Schlieffen mold to envelop and crush the enemy.[20]

Figure 28. German Second Army's leaders: Bülow, commander (left) and Lauenstein, chief of staff (right).

Leading the central force in the proposed battle, the Second Army, was the senior commander in the Prussian Army, *Generaloberst* Karl von Bülow (1846–1921). He was the scion of an ancient and prominent Prussian noble clan and brother of a former prime minister. More significantly Bülow was a highly-regarded General Staff officer who had played a major role in preparing the whole German Army for war. As was always the case with German field armies (and corps) in the First World War the responsibilities of command were partly shared with the Second Army's chief of staff, *Generalleutnant* (two-star) Otto von Lauenstein (1857–1916). Regulations required the commander to consult his chief of staff on all major decisions. In practice, it was very difficult for the commander to disregard his staff chief's advice.[21]

The German Third Army was essentially the Saxon Army: most of its forces were part of the Saxon Army, brought under central command at the outbreak of war. It was commanded by *Generalleutnant* Max Freiherr[*] von Hausen (1846–1922), the former Saxon Minister of War, with *Generalmajor* Ernst von Hoeppner (1860–1922) as his Chief of Staff. Hoeppner was a Prussian who did little to distinguish himself in that post but is remembered as one of the fathers of German air power for his later service as chief of the Army's Air Force (*Luftstreitkräfte*).

Part of the reason for the strong role of the chief of staff was that royal politics frequently played a major role in selecting army commanders. Some of the armies were commanded by royal princes while other top jobs were sometimes held by those with particularly good connections. (The Third Army was commanded by Hausen because none of the Saxon King's sons were of an age to command, even nominally.) At least one of these elite commanders was quite capable in his own right, but others weren't.

The exception to the usual rule that field army commanders were either royal or members of the General Staff was the leader of the First Army, *Generaloberst* Alexander von Kluck (1846–1934). He was the son of a commoner (a high-level civil servant) and does not seem

---

[*]   *Freiherr* was a title equivalent to Baron.

to have had any notable political connections.[*] He was the only non-royal army commander who had never attended the War Academy (*Kriegsakademie*) nor been a General Staff officer.

Figure 29. Kluck (wearing cloak), Kuhl (to his right), and staff officers of German First Army.

Bülow rushed more forces to the scene and ordered Kluck to wheel to the south and hit the French on their left flank. Kluck wanted to keep moving east in hopes of engaging the BEF and would later complain that Bülow's orders were all that had prevented him from annihilating it. In reality there were plenty of other obstacles. For instance, on August 23 poorly-planned communications arrangements caused one of Kluck's corps to receive a critical order too late to act on it and thus miss a major opportunity.[22]

In any event the coordinated blow Moltke had envisioned had turned into a ragged piecemeal advance. It was all in the glorious Prussian Army tradition of attacking whenever and wherever the opportunity arose but it seriously diminished any chance of enveloping and annihilating the French Fifth Army.

Any chance there may have been, that is, given that the German commanders had a seriously faulty understanding of the forces they were facing.

---

[*] Like many commoners who reached the top ranks, he was ennobled after becoming a general.

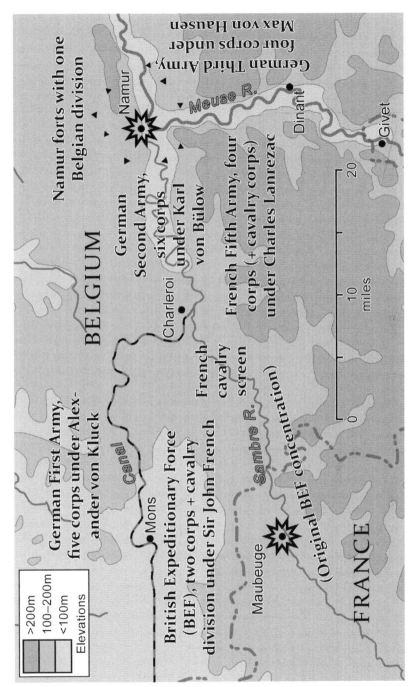

Figure 30. Battles of Mons, Charleroi, and Namur.

Both the Supreme Army HQ in Koblenz and Bülow thought that the British were only just advancing toward the area. Kluck believed they were closer but not yet in place.[23] They were all wrong; the British forces were just south of the canal on Kluck's left front. Incapable a commander as Sir John French was and limited as his forces were, stumbling over the BEF unawares was nonetheless bound to leave the Germans with some painful bruises.

On August 22 the main forces of Bülow's Second Army and Lanrezac's Fifth moved toward each other and started to engage in heavy fighting along the Sambre and to the south of it. Hausen's Third Army's attempts to cross the Meuse failed in the face of the strong natural obstacles and French fire (even though the defenses were thin) and thus it could do nothing to relieve the pressure on Bülow's forces. As Kluck's forces turned south they encountered signs that the BEF was nearby but some of the critical evidence didn't get reported up the line.

As the fighting continued on the 23rd, the French were forced back to the south. It was on that day too when German forces appeared in front of the British and launched attacks across the canal. Finally, on August 23 Hausen's Third Army managed to start crossing the Meuse. But because Lanrezac's troops had been pushed back so far by Bülow's, Hausen could not get around their flank.

That evening, first Lanrezac and then Sir John realized that they had no hopes of defeating or even continuing to resist the German forces they faced. They ordered their troops to break contact in the night and retreat.

After some hours Bülow, Kluck and Hausen realized that the enemy was retreating and set off in pursuit. In the meantime Bülow and Kluck sent messages to Molke congratulating themselves on their great and wonderful victory.

It was nothing of the kind. In strategic terms it was a large-scale skirmish in which they had inflicted considerable damage (and suffered some themselves) without changing the fundamental balance much. It was also the greatest lost opportunity of the war, the best chance the Germans would ever have of knocking out the French and their British allies. It they couldn't do it there, against an enemy inferior in every respect and who, (thanks especially to Sir John) deployed his forces in a very vulnerable position, then where could they?

If the three German field armies had annihilated the BEF and French Fifth Army as effective fighting forces, the position of the remaining French forces would have become desperate. They would have had a very strong German force on their left flank with nothing to stop it from rolling up their line. The French would have been forced to flee as quickly as possible to the southeast in hopes of finding defensive positions deep in the interior.

With the defeated forces instead largely intact the German right wing armies had to follow them in hopes of turning up other opportunities. They did, but none of those worked for them even as well as that along the Sambre had.

In Koblenz however there was general rejoicing. Along with equally exaggerated claims of victory from other German armies those from Kluck and Bülow created a great sense of euphoria. *The French were beaten! It could be only a matter of time before they collapsed or gave up! The war was all but won!*

As the fog of war was growing all but impenetrable on the 24th in Moltke's Headquarters, at Joffre's it was starting to clear a bit. Finally it was recognized that the Germans were both stronger and more capable than had been supposed and that the threat was far more serious than had been imagined. Joffre was known as a stubborn, deliberate, even staid commander who never did anything quickly, but now he turned on a sou. Corps were at once withdrawn from the armies on the right and center and entrained for Paris. Paris was France's main rail hub, served by direct lines from almost everywhere, and the greatest fortress in Europe. It could sustain and shelter an entire field army, and that was what Joffre assembled there late in August.

The strength of the German armies ebbed with each day's march to the south. In the heat of an especially hot August the First Army averaged 15 miles per day even counting the several days spent fighting, meaning that many units had to march significantly further. Boots and horseshoes wore thin, men and horses fell by the wayside. Lines of supply and reinforcement stretched ever longer. The forces further in toward the German left marched less but fought more and harder. The French and British too had exhausting marches but they were falling back along their supply lines, drawing nearer to their supply and replacement depots. And in many cases they could be transported on the intact rail network to their rear.

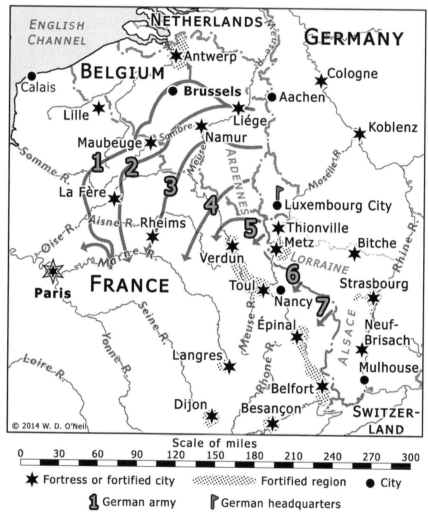

Figure 31. The German advance, to September 9.

In the meantime, on the 20th the German Eighth Army in East Prussia had lost its first battle against the Russians and was retreating. In dozens of war games and exercises the Germans had taken advantage of their central position and good railroads to shuttle troops from one front to another as the situation demanded, and now Moltke did just that, dispatching two corps to the East. At the same time he replaced the commander and chief of staff of the Eighth Army, the only major command changes he made.

By early September the Germans had reached the line of the Marne River stretching east of Paris. By then Joffre had assembled his new Sixth Army based around Paris and it marched out to attempt to roll up the German right wing, as the Germans had tried to do to the French left wing. It was no more successful than the Germans had been but with their worn-down forces the Germans found themselves in an awkward and increasingly vulnerable position. The German armies on the right and center were ordered to fall back to the next defensible line along the northern bank of the River Aisne.[*]

It was intended that the German armies would regroup and recover briefly before resuming the advance. In fact the two sides never moved far from the Aisne line until 1918 when, after a final fever-bed burst of offensive vigor, the German Army collapsed and Berlin sued for peace.

Chapter Summary

Efforts at the time to avoid blame for starting the war (plus later falsification of some records) have clouded understanding of events. In fact Russia first began mobilization in a way that directly threatened Germany (as well as Austria-Hungary). This was because the Russian high command feared their vulnerability to German attack if they moved against Austria-Hungary without forces mobilized near the German border. Concerned about their own defense if the Russians elected to use their mobilized forces to attack, after some delay and several warnings the German leaders announced mobilization and declared war on Russia.

At the same time (and without knowing of German actions) France too mobilized. The mobilization of French and Russian forc-

---

[*]   The series of actions along the line leading up to the German withdrawal is known as the (First) Battle of the Marne.

es triggered plans that called for simultaneous attacks on Germany as soon as sufficient forces were ready. They saw this combined offensive as an essential defensive measure, necessary to prevent the Germans from concentrating against one of them.

Similarly, the German plan, devised by the Great General Staff under the direction of *Generaloberst* (four-star general) Helmuth von Moltke the Younger (1848–1916)—nephew of the Moltke who had led the GGS and German Army to victory in the Wars of Unification—called for immediate invasion and conquest of Belgium in order to provide a path for a massive advance into northwestern France. This was seen as essential in order to clear Germany's western flank for long enough to move forces east to oppose the advancing Russian hordes. The route through Belgium allowed German forces to bypass the major obstacles and strong defenses in the southeast, but involved wholesale violation of Belgian neutrality.

The rapid advance through Belgium was made possible in part because at GGS insistence the Army had developed extra-powerful artillery to defeat fortresses, such as those that guarded critical transportation hubs in Belgium and France.

As they had agreed, the Russians and French invaded Germany while the German forces were still in Belgium, several days march from France. As part of the French offensive the Fifth Army under *Général* Charles Lanrezac advanced north into central Belgium, in the angle between the Meuse and Sambre Rivers, along a line between the towns of Namur and Charleroi. To their left and further to the north was arrayed the newly-arrived British Expeditionary Force (BEF) under Field Marshall Sir John French. The BEF formed the left of the Allied line, extending past the town of Mons, with a gap of about 70 miles between it and the sea.

The French and British here found themselves in the path of a powerful German force comprising the First Army under *Generaloberst* Alexander von Kluck, Second Army under *Generaloberst* Karl von Bülow, and Third Army under *Generalleutnant* Max Freiherr von Hausen. The Germans outnumbered the French-British force by 7:5 and had nearly twice the number of artillery pieces; moreover they were substantially more efficient, unit for unit. They were supposed to attack their foes on both flanks, cutting off their line of retreat. At the same time, attacks on the Franco-British front were to keep them in place while the outflanking maneuvers proceeded.

Success of this plan would have had catastrophic effects on the French, forcing the remainder of their armies elsewhere to flee deep into the south. The German forces had the strength to carry it out, exactly in accordance with doctrine. But it failed because the Germans lacked information about enemy dispositions and movements, could not coordinate their own efforts effectively, and were too slow to get behind the French and British before they could retreat. The French Fifth Army and BEF were hurt but could and did fight again.

In the same period French armies further to the southeast also were mauled and forced back.

During all this Moltke in the Supreme Army Headquarters in the rear was unable to get accurate information and had difficulty in communicating with the field army commanders. Other constraints prevented him from moving his headquarters closer to the scene. Because he was poorly informed he made some decisions he might have thought better of, given better information.

By early September the Germans had reached the line of the Marne River stretching east of Paris. But they were worn down and overextended. When the Allies launched a counteroffensive (known as the Battle of the Marne) the Germans fell back to the next river line to the north, that of the Aisne, intending to regroup and recover briefly before resuming the advance. In fact the two sides never moved far from the Aisne line until 1918 when after a final fever-bed burst of offensive vigor the German Army collapsed and Berlin sued for peace.

Figure 31 on page 88 provides an overview.

VII. Schlieffen's Daring Idea

MOST ACCOUNTS OF THE INITIAL stages of the war in the West say that the Germans were acting in accordance more or less with something the authors call "the Schlieffen Plan." But Chapter VI speaks only of Moltke's plans. This chapter takes up the question of the Schlieffen Plan and its relationship with the plans of Moltke, a relationship far less linear and straightforward than usually envisioned.

For decades the only real information historians had about the Great General Staff's planning came from what GGS veterans wrote about it. The actual documents were kept out of sight and then presumed destroyed in a World War II bombing raid. Some critical surviving documents were discovered and published in the 1950s but not until the 1990s did it become known that other important documents had survived in Russian and East German archives; it was several more years before all of them were available for study.

For reasons we'll explore later, what ex-GGS officers had written about the planning for World War I was misleading, so historians who took it at face value were in the dark. Only in the 2000s have deeply-researched explorations appeared, especially from military historian Terrence Zuber. Unfortunately, on top of their inherent complexity, Zuber presented them in ways sometimes tending to undermine his credibility among many historians.

Not only is the material dense and technical but it demands a thoroughgoing rethinking of much of what has long been taken to be fundamental about World War I and its origins. Few people welcome the news that substantial portions of their work have been built on a foundation of quicksand and will have to be fundamentally reconstructed on different ground, and it's natural to hope that it somehow really isn't so. That Zuber, no doubt quite frustrated, lectures them on their folly, compares their qualifications invidiously to his[*], and gloats in their discomfiture does nothing to diminish their resistance. Indeed, many people who have no prior stake and are approaching the issues with no established position find it natural to mistrust someone who trumpets the superiority of his work and dismisses as fools and mountebanks all who have gone before.[1]

All that aside, however, Zuber's work commands serious attention and respect, if with reservations on some points.[2]

. . .

THE SCHLIEFFEN OF THE Schlieffen Plan was the elder Moltke's successor as chief of the GGS, at one remove. Moltke stepped down in August 1888 at age 87 following the death of his master, Wilhelm I, and the accession of the old king's grandson, Wilhelm II. Moltke's deputy, Alfred von Waldersee (1832–1904), took over, having already run most of the day-to-day business of the GGS for some years. Like all top officials of the Empire the GGS chief served at the pleasure of the emperor, and Wilhelm II's pleasure was fickle. Waldersee had been a member of his circle but his plans did not please his master and in 1891 Waldersee was replaced with his deputy, Alfred Graf von Schlieffen[†] (1833–1913).[3]

Schlieffen had family connections throughout the top echelons of the Empire and moved easily in court and political circles to maintain and extend his influence. A widower, he lived with his two

---

[*]   Before getting his Ph.D. he was a mid-grade U.S. Army officer and had commanded an infantry company.

[†]   Again, "Graf" is a title rather than a part of Schlieffen's name. In his case it was hereditary from birth.

grown daughters in a spacious apartment on the top floor of the imposing new General Staff headquarters in the heart of Berlin, starting his work day at 6AM and finishing at midnight with time off only for riding and an hour with his daughters. Unlike Moltke who had cultural involvements, Schlieffen's sole "outside" interest was military history. He drove his staff hard but not as hard as he drove himself and they admired him for his dedication, knowledge and ideas.

Figure 32. Schlieffen.

Schlieffen carried on in the tradition of the elder Moltke and Waldersee, not simply trying to imitate them but to build on their work to develop new ideas and approaches. He focused particular attention on training and developing younger staff officers, imbuing them with his view of top-level doctrine and preparing them to function effectively and imaginatively at high levels in war. He continued the established practice of conducting "staff rides"—staff exercises in the field—twice each year plus war games in winter. In his hands they were not only very demanding training grounds but tools for exploring concepts and options, and for testing aspects of plans.

Sources differ on just how many General Staff officers there were, but more than 400 were needed to fill all of the general staffs for formations in the field when the army was mobilized, and hundreds more were required for the Supreme Army Headquarters so the total must have been somewhere excess of 500.[4]

Hundreds of them worked in the GGS in Berlin turning out a new set of war plans every April. The detail involved in planning every aspect of the mobilization, arming and equipment, provisioning and supply, transportation, concentration (*Aufmarsch*, which can also mean deployment) and initial direction of armies of millions of men was enormous. The core of the planning was the Military Transportation Plan, which minutely detailed the movement of more than 3 million men and 600,000 horses in 11,000 standardized unit trains over an interval of 312 hours from the start of mobilization, with provision for every need and contingency. It all was done by hand in an elaborately-organized, labor-intensive process. Without even civilian clerical workers to aid them the work absorbed the energies of most GGS officers. Nevertheless Schlieffen drew even officers at the lower levels of the GGS into his relentless pursuit of intellectual development and excellence.

. . .

AS SCHLIEFFEN REACHED HIS 70s the Kaiser, a quarter-century his junior, began thinking about a successor; his prerogative regardless of anyone else's wishes. The top army leadership did not align behind a single candidate, leaving Wilhelm a range of choices. Naturally he chose a man he knew, liked and respected, General Helmuth von Moltke—nephew and namesake of Moltke the Elder.[*][5]

The younger Moltke had grown up on his uncle's estate and came of age just in time to serve as a cadet and junior officer in the Franco-Prussian War, distinguishing himself in action. After the war he studied at the Prussian War Academy, the graduate school for training candidate General Staff officers, and then was appointed as a junior member of the GGS. In 1882 he became an adjutant to his famous uncle and continued in that role until the older man's death in 1891. By that time he knew everyone of importance in Wilhelmine Germany, including the Kaiser, who was taken with the tall, cultured, modest, personable, soldierly-looking officer with the famous

---

[*]   As nephew rather than son, he didn't inherit the Elder's title of Graf.

name and kept him on his staff from then on. Moltke commanded a battalion, a regiment, a brigade and then a division, but always in elite guards units near the palace and always while remaining an adjutant to the Kaiser.[6]

**Figure 33. The Kaiser at the 1904 maneuvers,
Moltke the Younger immediately behind him.**

Some saw this as meager preparation for heading the GGS but others believed it superior—and among them was the Kaiser. Schlieffen's ascetic intensity and sharp wit had gained him a devoted following of staff officers who were skeptical of his very different replacement. Moltke the Younger was no ascetic and showed few signs of exceptional brilliance. He was diligent and competent, and worked at refining, adjusting and improving plans for conflict, but although he was well liked as a person he gathered no coterie of admirers within the GGS.

As he left at the end of 1905, Schlieffen started to prepare a fairly detailed outline of how a campaign might be conducted in the west in order to rapidly annihilate the French Army in a one-front war. Schlieffen accurately labeled his memo as a "think piece" (*Denkschrift*) rather than a "plan," and both he and its later promoters were surely very well aware that it was not a war plan in any technical sense. It was a concept that was sometimes inconsistent, glossed over some very crucial details and relied on sweeping assumptions about what the enemy would do and not do.[7] Nevertheless it's been known as the "Schlieffen Plan" since at least 1920 and probably earlier.

The basic concept is often presented in the form of a map like Figure 34, which shows the axes of advance Schlieffen described.[*] As German forces mobilized they would move by rail to concentration areas along the entire French and Belgian borders but with by far the greatest mass opposite Belgium rather than France. These strong forces on the right wing would march rapidly through Belgium, reaching the phase line shown as M+21 by the 21st day after mobilization. (It's not clear whether these phase lines were laid down by Schlieffen or added by others.) On the left, along the border with France, only light forces would meet the expected French efforts to reconquer the lost Alsace-Lorraine provinces.

The right wing would march on into Northern France reaching the M+30 line by the 30th day after mobilization. The forces far on the right would continue down the coast and circle Paris to wrap completely around the French and smash them against the German defenses along the border with France as well as the neutral Swiss border. In this way the French were to be annihilated as an effective fighting force and compelled to give up.

The map really can only show one possible outcome and as Schlieffen always emphasized strongly, nothing in war is really calculable. It shows the desired result in what Schlieffen thought of as the most likely situation. Nothing at all is said in the memo regarding the Russians, and the campaign it describes not only absorbs all of Germany's planned forces but considerably more from sources not identified. It's a concept for a war in which a greatly strengthened

---

[*]   Other "Schlieffen Plan" maps depict a rather different pattern of operations. I referred closely to what Schlieffen wrote as well as the maps that accompanied his memo in drawing this, attempting to summarize his points and bring them to life without distorting them.

Germany somehow did not have to worry at all about Russia even to
the extent of keeping a covering force in the east.

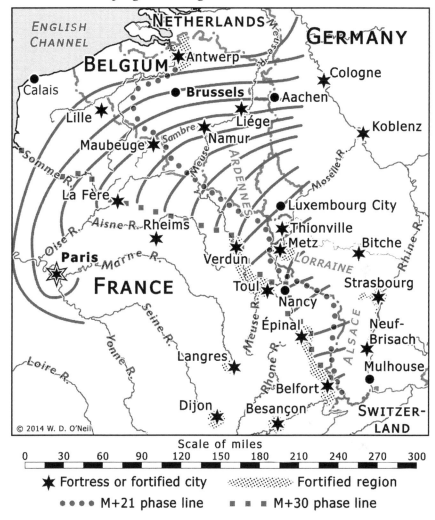

Figure 34. The "Schlieffen Plan," 1906.

This, the former GGS officers insisted after Germany's defeat,
was the culmination of Schlieffen's genius, the end point of years of
thought and testing that led straight to the memo. Regardless of
what they thought about the substance of the plan, historians all
took this to be an accurate description of how it evolved. That is they
did until Zuber's research in the archives cast serious doubt on every

aspect of the story. What Schlieffen did and said in the years before the "Great Memorandum" related to it in no more than indirect and tangential ways, if that.

Zuber also has shown that the plan had no very distinct effect on Moltke's planning or war-gaming between 1906 and 1914 which continued largely in the mold of Schlieffen's actual planning and war-gaming with some modifications and adjustments.[8] In 1911, five years after it was written (and while Schlieffen was still alive and active) Moltke re-read (or read) it and added some comments in a generally rather skeptical tone. There's no record that Schlieffen ever complained that his putative masterpiece was being ignored.

The think-piece was an often-used bureaucratic device, as it still is. Sometimes it was intended straightforwardly to advance and promote a particular policy. Often however such memos served as stalking horses to help make or refute some argument, perhaps one only tenuously related to the ostensible object. What we know of Schlieffen and his methods does not suggest that we ought necessarily to assume that he was arguing straightforwardly.

Zuber has said that the memo was really intended to argue for a larger army, to be gained by conscripting a larger portion of the eligible young men. Schlieffen had complained for years that while France conscripted about four-fifths of her young men—essentially all who were fit to serve—for Germany the fraction was little over half. The memorandum showed that Germany was unlikely to be able to defeat France in an offensive campaign without a substantially larger army and Zuber believes that this was meant to be used by Moltke as an argument for larger conscription totals.

It's fair to say that few people other than Zuber have ever found this idea especially convincing. Schlieffen had never had any success with his desultory proposals for more men made while he was in office. Can he really have supposed that a long, complex, and abstract treatise on how to fight an offensive war against France, delivered by a successor who was far from being in full agreement with him, would have greater effect? It's not entirely out of the question, of course. Perhaps he felt that the obstacles that had prevented him from gaining a major change in Army strength (and indeed had in-

hibited him from ever trying terribly hard) would not apply to Moltke, and perhaps he believed that his think piece would somehow
stiffen Moltke's resolve or provide him with ammunition. But if so it
was more a wild hope than the sort of rational plan he was renowned
for.

There were two fundamentally different ways for Germany to approach a war with France. One would be to await a French attack and
then counterattack. That was the approach Schlieffen and Moltke
played in the great majority of their exercises and war games. The
"Schlieffen Plan" memo represents the opposite approach of invading France and attacking her army.

The arguments in favor of and against both approaches will be
probed later, but the point here is that they were quite different, and
that Schlieffen had little record of favoring the strategy of the offensive rather than counterattack. Some authors argue that he changed
his mind in response to increased tensions with France and anxieties
about the adequacy of a counteroffensive strategy.[9] There's no direct
evidence against that thesis, but there's none in support of it either;
it's all unsupported inference.[10]

There's another inference we might draw. The concept laid out in
Schlieffen's memo outlining an offensive war against France required
a minimum of 96 divisions in the west, implying a need to expand
the German Army by a quarter over its actual 1914 strength (assuming minimal forces in the east). Ninety-six divisions didn't guarantee
success but fewer than 96 made failure very likely.[11] This might be
taken to imply that Schlieffen wrote the memorandum as a caution
against adopting an offensive strategy or at least against doing so
without thoroughly working out what was needed to implement it
(as he had earlier worked out what was necessary for the counteroffensive strategy) and making adequate preparations. The preparations had to include creating enough divisions, although it will be
shown later that it would take more than just that.

We don't actually know what Schlieffen's real intention was and
probably never will. It's certain, however, that his 1906 think-piece
was not a plan, not in the military sense of a specific blueprint for
action. We can be sure because it had scarcely any of the infor

mation needed to make a usable war plan.[*] It wasn't even a statement of commander's intent since when it was written Schlieffen's days as a commander were over. In fact it was a set of ideas about a possible course of action and speculations about how it might work out.

. . .

ZUBER HAS REPEATEDLY INSISTED, "There never was a 'Schlieffen Plan.'"[12] That is, there was a Schlieffen memo but it was never made into a plan and the plans that were made didn't reflect it.

So how then has the "Schlieffen Plan" come to occupy a central place in the historiography of the initial phase of World War I?

Schlieffen's memo was kept from sight until Germany's defeat in 1945, but various official and semi-official historians were allowed access and permitted to write about it in the 1920s and 1930s—all former General Staff officers. Most depicted it as an admonition from the genius Schlieffen to his less-gifted successor about how to win the war—a plan that would have brought victory if Moltke had followed it. Moltke, they intimated, had tried to follow it but was too dimwitted and lacking in "will," and so bungled it.

The Second Army and its commander, Bülow as well as his chief of staff Lauenstein, also came in for some lumps for not having pushed hard enough to carry out the Schlieffen Plan. And *Oberstleutnant* (Lieut. Colonel) Richard Hentsch (1869–1918), whom Moltke used as an observer and emissary to the out-of-touch right-wing army headquarters, was assailed for having either exceeded his orders or followed them too slavishly.

All four of these men, Moltke, Bülow, Lauenstein and Hentsch, shared an important common characteristic—they were no longer around to offer any corrections, having died of illnesses exacerbated by the stresses of war.

In some cases the critics were no doubt at least partly motivated by desire to deflect blame from themselves. But not all can well be accused of this and particularly not *General der Infanterie* (three-star

---

[*]   I should remark that I've been a war planner in a professional capacity and have a clear idea of what is needed. —W. D. O'Neil

general) Wilhelm Groener (1867–1939), who bore no responsibility for Moltke's plans. Before the war Groener's time at the GGS had been spent in planning the railroad schedules for mobilization and working with railroad companies and authorities to ensure that Army needs would be met when the time came. It was an immense, extremely important task, but it did not involve him in the planning of strategy.

Figure 35. Groener, 1916.[13]

When the war began Groener, still a mid-grade officer, was assigned responsibility for all military railroad operations in the west, a very challenging job that he performed extremely well. For a while in 1917 Groener commanded an infantry division fighting on the Western Front and then took command of a corps on the Eastern Front (where the fighting was nearing its end) before serving as chief of staff in a field army. But for much of the war he held a unique position as the man responsible for expanding war production, reporting to *General der Infanterie* Erich Ludendorff (1865–1937), who by August 1916 was Germany's virtual military dictator. It was after stepping on too many toes that Groener got sent to the field.[14]

By October 1918 Ludendorff was visibly in collapse, with the Empire not far behind him. There was already an established pattern of calling Groener in when there were seemingly unsolvable problems and so he replaced Ludendorff, with virtually unlimited powers.

Back in Berlin, in the space of a few weeks Groener pushed the Kaiser off into abdication and exile, made deals that preserved the country from civil war while installing a constitutional government, and supported peace on the best terms Germany could get, before seeing to the peaceful and orderly demobilization of the nation's armies. All in all a pretty remarkable record for a man who had been born the son of a common soldier and paymaster in the Württemberg Army and had no connections or influence to aid his rise.

Although the GGS was largely meritocratic by the early 1900s and had many non-noble officers, Groener's origins were especially plebian and not even Prussian. He was enough of an outsider to constrain his pre-war career horizons.[15] After the war he was viewed with some suspicion and disdain by many of his fellow former General-Staff officers as the man who had fired the Kaiser, installed a civilian government, accepted the Versailles peace terms, and perhaps especially had dealings with the Social Democrats.[*] He and Ludendorff in particular differed on virtually everything but the time of day.

Notwithstanding his deep reservations about liberal democratic governments, Groener accepted a series of high offices in the Weimar Republic in the 1920s. The victorious Allies had forced Germany to disband the General Staff at least on paper but Groener used his political power to allocate the functions and many of the officers of the GGS among various government organizations and to ensure that officers of the abolished General Staff got the top places in the shrunken Army. In short, he was the principal institutional post-war protector of the General Staff.

Very likely it seemed important to Groener to deflect accusations that the General Staff had lost the war and indeed gotten Germany into a war it didn't know how to win in the first place. There were various ways he might have approached this. Ludendorff for instance laid Germany's defeat at the feet of the Freemasons, Jesuits, the Vatican, degenerates, socialists, liberals—and of course Jews—

---

[*]   They were the majority political party but nevertheless unacceptable to many officers. Groener had no love for them, but was a political realist.

who he claimed had conspired to "stab Germany in the back," undoing all the efforts of her heroic army and brilliant General Staff.

But Groener despised this *Dolchstoß* or stab-in-the-back theory and despised Ludendorff for pushing it (as well as for playing footsie with the Nazis, and just on general principle). As an alternative Groener might have insisted that the GGS had been forced to make bricks without straw as a result of the refusal of the pre-war politicians to respond to its repeated calls for increases in the strength of the Army. Or he could have blamed diplomatic fumbles that left Germany standing alone and all but friendless amidst a host of enemies. He might well have chosen to pin a great deal of the blame on Ludendorff himself, for he had not only been Germany's military dictator in all but name for much of the war but had played a prominent part in formulating the plans executed in 1914.

Instead, Terrence Zuber says, Groener and others, "invented the Schlieffen Plan in order to protect the reputation of the general staff," and claimed that "had the younger Moltke only followed it, the Germans would have beaten the French in a manner [*sic*] of weeks."[16] That is, the core of Groener's defense of the General Staff was that the acuteness of one of its chiefs had been subverted by the obtuseness of another. It's hard to believe that Groener picked this story out of a cynical calculation that it was the most effective and fireproof defense of the institution both had headed that the mind of man could devise. It should have taken no great genius to foresee that it could very well be used to indict rather than defend the General Staff, as indeed it has been by historian Hans Delbrück in Groener's own time and by Gerhard Ritter and many followers since.

The real reason that Groener chose it, it seems, is that he believed it to be true or at least that it had some foundation in truth. For despite what Zuber says about the story having been invented in the 1920s, there is definite evidence that Groener saw the spirit of Schlieffen at work in Moltke's plans for the advance to the Marne at least as early as August 1914, as it was in progress when he was observing it at first hand as an *Oberstleutnant* and the railroad and transportation chief under Moltke in the German Army headquarters, first in Koblenz and then after August 29 in Luxembourg City.

Groener dealt constantly with the rail transportation demands resulting from movements of the armies and he was the sort of person who talked with everyone in the Supreme Army Headquarters and heard about everything that was going on. He must have watched the big headquarters situation map closely and seen the operations of Figure 31 as they unfolded day by day. He wrote in his diary and to his wife about the wonderful Schlieffen-inspired operations then underway on the Western Front. At first he was exultant, later despairing, but always credited the concept of the operations to Schlieffen. To be sure Groener didn't refer to "the Schlieffen Plan" and it's unlikely that he had ever seen the closely-held memo of 1906 at that time.[7] But he spoke of victory "à la Schlieffen," of "Schlieffen beatings" of the French, of "Schlieffen's spirit in all the operations." He referred to Schlieffen as "the man who thought up all the ideas we are carrying out."[8]

On September 5, as cracks were growing too wide to ignore, Groener confided to his diary,

> Hopefully the armies' uncontrolled advances will now stop in the west and we will begin a period of calm war-making, in order to bring about a crushing victory.
>
> In my opinion, the uncontrolled advances of the Fourth and Fifth Armies were not in accordance with the idea that formed the basis of all the operations through Belgium....
>
> [The GGS operations section chief] spoke several times about the brutal force with which the operations had to be executed. — I believe a little less brutality and instead ordering the armies in the middle in the Schlieffen sense would have produced greater successes.[19]

And on September 13, after the Germans had retreated from the Marne River, Zuber wrote in his diary,

> The "plan" of the late Schlieffen has been temporarily misplaced. Perhaps it will be found again.[20]

There we see the core of the criticism Groener would level after the war already expressed even before the failure became final and unmistakable. We cannot truly be sure what motivated his criticisms after the war but they only elaborated on ideas formed a decade before.

VIII. The Flaws of the Perfect Plan

AFTER IT WAS ALL OVER, after the army they had led had been defeated and disgraced, after the Kaiser to whom they had sworn
their loyalty had scuttled away from the shadow of the gallows, after
the nation they were charged to protect had been ground into the
muck and rent by political paroxysms, and after their institution had
been formally condemned and abolished, former officers of the former Great General Staff sought to explain how it could all have gone
so catastrophically wrong.

Others chimed in but they lacked crucial information, including
much that has only recently come into public view thanks to patient
historical research, principally by Zuber.

There were some disagreements but scarcely anyone doubted
that the plan for conducting the war in the West had been drawn
from Schlieffen's 1905/1906 Great Memorandum. Aside from civilian
commentators like Delbrück, who had to rely on second-hand information from General Staff officers, Zuber sees this unanimity as
evidence of a conspiracy orchestrated by Groener and/or Kuhl.

Those with extensive experience in secret matters will wonder.
It's usually possible to get a number of suitably motivated people all
to keep silent regarding some critical piece of information, such as
the existence of a program to develop a terrible new weapon, the

means of collecting intelligence information or the particulars of a planned attack, whose importance they all recognize. But to get them uniformly to repeat the same cover story is all but impossible and at very best requires an elaborate and inherently insecure apparatus of coordination.

The men who spoke of the Schlieffen Plan as the foundation of the invasion of Belgium and France may have coordinated some details but it's very hard to see how they could have written and said what they did unless they truly agreed about the basics of the story.[1]

. . .

SCHLIEFFEN MADE A SUITABLE ICON. Kuhl had spent more than seven years as a section chief under him. Ludendorff had served nearly four years under him. Groener had started in the General Staff under Schlieffen. Almost regardless of the capacity an officer had served in and duration of contact Schlieffen seems to have made a powerful impression. For Groener and many others Schlieffen was the archetype of the *Feldherr*—the adamantine, commanding, all-seeing, infinitely resourceful, god-like lord of the battlefield in the mold of Frederick the Great or Napoléon.

The younger Moltke, whatever his merits might perhaps have been, had lost his great gamble in the first six weeks of war. He couldn't possibly be a *Feldherr*—true *Feldherren* were winners.

Figure 34 shows what Schlieffen laid out in his memorandum, while in Figure 31 we see what actually happened. In Figure 36 the two maps have been laid side-by-side to bring out the similarities and differences, with some cropping and editing to ensure that they can be read at this smaller size. (Remember that the lines in the maps have different meanings. In the right-hand map they represent specific field armies while on the left they're simply flowlines of the directions of movement in general.)

It's evident that the right-hand panel of Figure 36 resembles the left but only very broadly. In the left panel Schlieffen has the great German bear lunge out through Belgium to swiftly sweep up the French armies in his powerful right paw and crush them against his chest and the Swiss Alpine rock on his left.

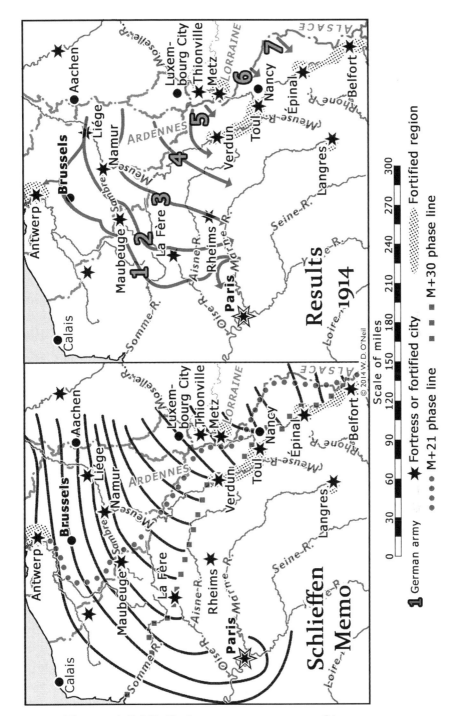

Figure 36. Schlieffen's concept vs. events of August 1914.

But in 1914 the German force was a billy goat repeatedly butting the French southward, doing a lot of damage but never delivering an annihilating blow and ultimately exhausting himself. Butting plainly wasn't what Groener thought Moltke was trying to do at the time, nor what Moltke envisioned either. Exactly what he had in mind isn't known with certainty but it appears that it had at least major elements of a Schlieffen bear-hug. That's presumably why Groener and others he knew in the headquarters spoke of the plan as having been inspired by Schlieffen. What's known of what he said and did at the time indicates that Moltke saw a real chance that his armies could effectively knock France out of the war at least for many weeks relatively quickly by surrounding and defeating hers. So it's reasonable enough to speak of him as having pursued *a* partly Schlieffen-like plan (but not *the* Schlieffen Plan) and as having failed to pull it off.

The main flaw, as Groener's diagnosis went, lay in not putting all available troops in the right half of the line stretching along the Belgian frontier north from Thionville. This meant there weren't enough men to overlap the French to the west and turn their flank. Major contributory problems were that Moltke lacked the will and intellect of the true *Feldherr*, failed to give his army commanders firm direction and didn't effectively insist that they follow the direction he did give them. And they weren't fit to be *Feldherren* either.

. . .

WHILE SOMEWHAT MORE might have been done with the forces in hand, in reality there was no chance whatever that they could have reached far enough for Schlieffen's grand sweep around Paris. He'd thought about this as insurance against what actually happened in 1914—stretching of the French defensive line all the way to the vast rail hub and fortress of Paris. But even with all the forces Germany had and all that anyone could imagine might be raised, there would never have been enough for this maneuver. Moreover, there wasn't even room in Belgium and Northern France to have accommodated them if they had existed.

A few simple calculations help make this point more concrete. when mobilization was complete in mid-August the Army had 39 corps, including 14 reserve formations, which all took much the same road space. In addition there were 11 cavalry divisions for service with the field armies, plus 10 infantry divisions for second- and third-line duties, and a number of miscellaneous units. Of the 39 corps 34, or 87 percent, were on the Western Front. Twenty-six corps marched with the five field armies arrayed north of Thionville, representing two-thirds of the total Army strength and three-quarters of the corps strength on the Western Front. Seven of the Army's eleven independent cavalry divisions also rode with the right-wing field armies.[2]

To be able to deploy for battle within a day of contacting an enemy force a field army's corps should ideally march on parallel roads 10 to 15 miles apart. Thus the 26 right-wing corps needed a corridor of at least 270 miles—but they only had only about half of that available to them, a part of which lay in the rugged Ardennes where roads were few and the going slow. The two rightmost armies with 12 corps needed at least 130 miles and again had only about half that. The resulting crowding reduced readiness for combat and also generated frictions that slowed progress and impeded supply. It's part of why Bülow and Kluck couldn't exert enough of their potential strength quickly enough to crush the French and British at Charleroi and Mons on August 21-24. Stuffing more troops into the limited space available would have made it all worse and eventually would have choked movement and supply altogether.[3]

And to encircle Paris the troops on the right wing in Figure 34 needed a clear path and adequate supply. They would have had to march well over 400 miles (allowing 15 percent extra to account for the fact that roads do not run straight in the direction you want to go). If they could maintain a steady pace of 15 miles every day this would take them 4 weeks. Since they could not start until August 17, the final position shown on the right panel of Figure 36 would not be reached before mid-September, 45 days or so after August 2, the first day of mobilization. What were the French going to be doing in all that time? Waiting for the bear to close his paw around them? Most likely they would have had time to retire south, to areas around Langres or the Loire River.

Have you ever walked 15 miles? Under a load of more than 50 pounds of weapons, ammunition, clothing, and gear?[4] In blazing heat? Day after day for four weeks without a break? It can be done—by robust, highly motivated young men in good physical condition, well accustomed to walking long distances. Even of them, however, a considerable number would fall by the wayside due to physical problems for at least a day or two and have somehow to catch up or trail along behind. And afterward no one would be fully fit for arduous combat without several days of rest.

We could go on in this vein, but the obvious lesson is that even with a lot more troops and resources available Schlieffen's great sweep to the west was not a practical proposition, not something that even a pretty daring commander could really count on. All the will in the world cannot change the limits of time, space and distance, nor human and animal endurance.

Thus Groener's confidence in Schlieffen's concept was ill-founded. If its success depended on a sweep around Paris then it couldn't succeed.

But that's not to say that Groener's other criticisms are irrelevant, for Moltke's semi-Schlieffen plan might possibly have succeeded with better execution and a few more breaks. And with more foresight and preparations its chances could have been improved.

IX. Making It Work—Maybe

REGARDLESS OF WHAT WE CHOOSE to call it, and of exactly what we envision its objectives to have been, there is no getting around the conclusion that the German plan for war in the west failed to work. Some people take that to mean that the Germans were incompetent fools who risked everything on an impossible plan while others see it as a plan that "should" have worked except for bad luck or the personal failings of Moltke.

This chapter argues that: (1) Moltke's plan might have worked with enough luck. (2) Once the war had begun neither Moltke nor anyone else had many options for making the plan work better. (3) If the problems had been adequately thought through beforehand there were practical ways to improve the chances of success.

The Germans benefitted from a good deal of luck in August 1914. First it was the earliest date at which the giant 420 mm siege howitzers were available in a form suitable for road transport. Without them it might have taken another week or more to capture the Belgian forts, setting back the whole schedule and giving the British and French much more time to respond.

Moreover it was August rather than some other time of year. That meant the enervating misery of marching long distances in cloudless heat but also mudless roads and food to eat along the way.

By mid-August the harvest had been brought in with most of its produce still stored in the villages and towns, not yet shipped. Not many weeks earlier or later the armies would have had much more difficulty in eating off the land, putting substantial additional strain on the supply system.

Figure 37. Trains could move heavy loads 200 miles or more per day, but only where the main lines ran. Wagons were more flexible, but made less than 20 miles per day.

The supply system was already very strained, and it could have been far worse. The only way to ship large quantities of supplies and matériel in 1914 was by rail—Belgian and French rails. The Belgians and French had plans to wreck their railroad tunnels and bridges so badly that the lines would have taken months to reopen, but under the hectic pressure of the rapid German advance actual demolitions were spotty. They were enough to present problems for the Germans but workarounds were found. It was arduous but the German logisticians were able to get adequate supplies to the troops, only just barely.[1]

The weakness of French demolitions was related to the biggest piece of luck for Germany: for nearly three weeks, until August 24, the French high command resolutely ignored all the evidence of a massive German advance through Belgium and Northern France. Joffre, the French commander, was doing his own billy-goat act, launching his forces to batter against the Germans in Eastern France and dismissing all reports of trouble looming in the northwest.

But then Madame Fortune tired of being taken for granted. On the 24th Joffre suddenly started acting like the *Feldherr* that Groener and his colleagues lamented the lack of. Moltke needed a plan that could succeed even if the French woke up, and he didn't have one. With his right wing resting on a belt of strong fortifications and good intact rail lines running directly to Paris, Joffre was able to shift large forces to the capital, west of the maximum reach of Kluck's First Army.

And as pointed out on page 86 the Germans had missed their greatest opportunity just about the time that Joffre was realizing he had a problem, when Kluck's First Army and Bülow's Second, together with Hausen's Third, failed to annihilate Lanrezac's Fifth Army and Sir John French's BEF west of Namur. The German forces outnumbered their opponents, had much stronger artillery, were better trained and had better tactics—but could not defeat them decisively.

The fundamental reason was that the German forces never were able to exert their advantage in strength at all fully. They couldn't find their opponents quickly enough and couldn't coordinate the actions of their various formations and commands in response to the information they did gain. And even when finally they knew where the enemy was and got everyone on the same course they simply couldn't get their troops around the flanks quickly enough to prevent the French and British from slipping away.

In 1940, at the outset of another World War, the Germans had better reconnaissance and communications to direct armored and motorized divisions with the mobility and agility to outmaneuver the French and British. That wasn't possible in 1914.

Mobility

OR WAS IT? THERE WEREN'T any tanks in 1914 but there were trucks. The German Army had a few thousand of them in August 1914— enough to be very important for getting ammunition and critical supplies to the front at the right flank but not enough (and certainly not organized enough) to make a real operational difference. With some foresight and preparation it could have been different, critically different.

It had taken the early auto industry a decade or so to develop the technologies for heavy vehicles but by 1905 motor buses were becoming common in city streets and very quickly trucks came into widespread use, first for local delivery and then increasingly for heavy industrial and agricultural haulage.[2]

German military interest in trucks sprouted quite early. In a sense, it had developed well before trucks had. Inventors had been building experimental road vehicles and tractors powered by steam since the 1760s and by the 1850s commercial models were in use. In the 1870-71 war with France the Prussian Army employed two 40 ton 20 horsepower agricultural steam tractors. They were useful within their limits but the limits were too restrictive to encourage wide use. Nevertheless such experiences led officers to speculate about what might be done with better vehicles.

By about 1905 trucks had assumed a reasonably efficient form suitable for wide use. Layouts were much like those of modern trucks with ladder frames and front-mounted engines driving rear wheels. The engines usually had outputs of no more than 60 horsepower but their design gave them good low-speed torque for high pulling power. Transmissions and running gear were primitive but they served for vehicles with little power and low speed. Makers were not yet able to build pneumatic tires adequate for heavy weights so trucks ran on solid rubber tires mounted directly on the rims. That and crude suspensions limited speeds but the roads of the day weren't up to high-speed traffic anyway. Large military convoys have to drive slowly in any event but ten miles per hour was a lot faster than men could march and faster even than horses could move except for brief spurts. Convoys also make more efficient use of road space; although they stretch out over a long distance in order to maintain adequate intervals between trucks, they move fast enough to more than compensate.

Before World War I, a three- to four-ton truck suitable for military use cost about $3,000 to $3,500 complete with basic equipment—the equivalent of roughly $55,000 to $65,000 in 2013 terms.[3]

That doesn't seem like all that much to us—not too much more than the 2013 average per-capita GDP in the United States. But at the time the price of a truck amounted to about ten times the average German per-capita GDP.[4] The effect of this was that before the war the price of a truck could buy roughly eight times as much labor as it does today. If it was a purely economic tradeoff a truck had to save a lot of manpower to be worthwhile.

Trucks were actually cheaper to buy and run than horses at least for many kinds of uses.[5] But the Army saved by keeping only limited forces of draft horses in peacetime, only enough to move a portion of artillery and wagons for training. With agriculture depending almost entirely on animal traction and with horse-drawn wagons and individual mounts far outnumbering motor vehicles on German roads the country had millions of horses and there were provisions to buy hundreds of thousands quickly on mobilization. Thus the cost of horses was minimized except when they were needed.

If horses could be mobilized as needed, why not trucks? One problem was that there simply weren't so many trucks to mobilize. Although German firms had bought trucks at an increasing rate in the recovery from the 1907 depression, by 1914 there were still only 9,639 registered trucks and another 907 buses.[6]

With GGS prompting, the War Ministry had instituted a scheme to encourage firms to buy trucks suited to hauling ammunition by providing a subsidy. Accepting it made the truck liable to be called up upon mobilization but of course, the odds were that most trucks of any kind would be pressed into service (as happened in 1914). The scheme was enacted in 1908 and by 1914 more than 800 subsidy trucks were available.[7]

**Figure 38. Typical medium and heavy subsidy trucks.
Truck convoys could cover 75 miles or more in a day.**

The few thousand trucks the German Army was able to gather up in 1914, supplemented by a few thousand more seized in Belgium and France, were crucially important in moving ammunition from railheads scores of miles behind the advancing troops up to the front, but there weren't nearly enough of them to take over the duties of very many of the hundreds of thousands of horses that marched with Germany's armies.

Simply replacing more horse-drawn supply wagons with trucks would have done little to make the Schlieffen Plan more feasible. For that it would have been necessary to carry troops in trucks. This was exactly what was done on a large scale by 1918. (Only by the Allies, since German industry, weakened by the lack of imported raw materials, was unable to produce enough trucks.) Trucks weren't fundamentally better than in 1914; the difference was that in 1918 the French and British had about 85,000 of them on the Western Front but no one had even a tenth that many in 1914.[8]

In fact during the pursuit of the French forces retreating to the south in late August 1914 some German infantry was carried in trucks in an effort to catch them. There weren't enough trucks to do it on the scale needed and the results aren't recorded.[9]

There was also the famous incident of the "taxicabs of the Marne," about 500 taxis (and buses) pressed into service to carry two infantry regiments from Paris to the front at Nanteuil on September 7-8. Other forces traveled by truck. There were many problems but the troops got there and much was learned.[10]

To motorize two corps (85,000 men) with their artillery and equipment the Germans would have needed about 12,000 trucks (judging by later experience). On the relatively good Belgian and French main roads the motorized troops would have been able to advance 75 miles or more per day, or twice that in short-term emergencies. This was slower than rail but five times as fast as foot formations moved, meaning that motorized formations could have outmaneuvered French foot armies. Despite tremendous exertions the German First and Second Armies never managed to get around the flank of the Allied left wing, but with two motorized corps they almost certainly could have, or armies elsewhere could have found or created gaps for motorized formations to exploit. Two corps should have been sufficient for a very major impact. This would be particularly so as trucks could run back to pick up reinforcements relatively rapidly.

The trucks would be very vulnerable to fire from artillery, machine guns or massed infantry. They would need to stay a minimum of five miles from enemy forces, with the infantry advancing the final distance on foot. Nevertheless, the motorized infantry would be able to attack more swiftly than the enemy could bring in reinforcement, and with not so far to march they could carry heavier weapons and ammunition loads. When on the move the column of trucks would need to be supported by frequent air patrols, and be preceded by a strong and ready advance guard.

To buy, operate, maintain, and progressively replace 12,000 vehicles would have cost the Army about $18 million each year in the dollars of that day (about $200 million in the 1990 dollars of Figure 9), adding as much as eight percent to the pre–1912 Army budget.* Raising the Army budget from 3.5 to 3.8 percent of GDP wouldn't have crippled Germany, and if spent on the new technology of trucks in fact might well have stimulated the economy enough to pay for itself.

Practical politics was another matter. The price of getting all the German states and statelets to agree to empire in 1871 had included promising them considerable power over budgets. And the popularly-elected Parliament (*Reichstag*), with which that power was shared, had become a monster, resistant to the control of the Kaiser and his lieutenants. The officials of the 1900s lacked the ferociously intimidating combativeness and tactical adeptness of Bismarck, and preferred to avoid confrontation.

Moreover, allocating eight percent of an increased Army budget to acquisition of hardware would have represented a major break

---

*   This assumes purchase of 3,000 trucks each year at a cost of $3,000 apiece, plus a similar sum for operations and maintenance, in line with the prices of the day and a great deal of subsequent operating experience with similar systems. In practice, the cost of trucks would have declined over time due to high production rates.

with existing patterns of spending. Even in peacetime, the bulk of Army funding went to personnel and operating expenses.* Another eight percent on the acquisition side of the budget would have seemed like a significant distortion to many.[11]

But there was a very obvious precedent for spending on motorization, and a ready source: the *Kaiserliche Marine*, the Imperial German Navy. Germany had no need or use for a big-league navy; geography decreed that her economic, political, and strategic fate was going to be played out on land, with no more than a minor role for purely local sea power. Nevertheless, a complex of enthusiasms stimulated the Kaiser and his realm to plunge on deep-water naval spending in the early 1900s—$50 million to $110 million every year.[12]

Advanced warships were a high-technology product and the building program did something to strengthen German industry, but not along lines that meshed especially well with Germany's overall commercial position. It was entirely predictable that the more than $800 million spent on the Navy in the decade before World War I would do Germany very little good in a war against Britain and would help make a conflict with the world's greatest sea power more likely—and so it proved. Germany would have been better off banking the money.

And better off still to have spent it on motorizing substantial ground forces. It's reasonable to suppose that the Kaiser might have liked such an idea, that industrial and labor interests would have seen much in it for them and that it could have attracted public enthusiasm. Like any such proposal it could have failed but it would have been well worth trying. All that would have been necessary to have set the whole thing in motion would have been for Moltke to have presented it to the Kaiser. He had a longstanding close personal relationship with the monarch that would have permitted him to make the case privately.[13] One of the few things Wilhelm II truly was

---

* Seventy years later, in a period when armies had become much more technological, the U.S. Army spent less than 22 percent of its budget on acquisition of matériel. (Averaged over fiscal years 1975–1980, a time of low operational pace.)

good at was promotion; if his enthusiasm could have been captured the proposal would have been well on its way.

This was not a role that was foreign to the Great General Staff. Schlieffen, Moltke and the GGS had exercised a major influence in revolutionizing German artillery over the 15 years before the war, to Germany's great advantage. They also played central parts in prompting development of air forces and machine gun troops.

Any really serious analysis of ideas for large-scale envelopment of the French armies could scarcely fail to lead to the conclusion that if Joffre played his hand at all prudently it probably could not be done without some advantage in mobility at the operational level, the level of corps and armies. Motor vehicles were the only logical way to do this and there was no need to wonder what they were like—they were rolling by the GGS building in Berlin at Königsplatz and Moltkestrasse all the time.

The GGS did ask for trucks—they were a driving force behind the subsidy truck program—but only to carry ammunition and provide traction for heavy artillery. It was a major missed opportunity.

Reconnaissance

THERE WERE DAYS WITH EARLY fog and some rain storms but on the whole the weather was hot and dry over Western Europe that August—so much so as to draw comment. It was hard on men and horses marching at their fastest pace, and torment for those lying wounded and without water in the field.

It wasn't good for the airships that the French and especially the Germans were relying on for strategic reconnaissance; the heat reduced their lifting capacity and the turbulence it generated endangered their landings and takeoffs.

But it kept the roads dry and firm and it was favorable for flying airplanes. That was fortunate for commanders, who found themselves depending on the new machines—far more so than they had imagined.

Before 1914 most commanders on all sides expected large cavalry forces to tell them where the enemy was and what he was doing. They also depended on the horsemen to prevent the enemy from getting the same information about them. Clearly, some were going to lose out.

The Germans generally believed that they could see without being seen. After all their cavalry was magnificently trained and well mounted, and the heirs to an ancient and glorious tradition. It was all true and it wasn't enough. German cavalry did a pretty good job, on the whole, of blocking enemy reconnaissance and locating enemy screening forces. But they could very rarely penetrate the enemy's screens to determine the real strength, movements and dispositions of the forces (if any) beyond them.[14]

As mentioned on pages 39-42 the Great General Staff was enthusiastic about airplanes. They battled with the War Ministry's Zeppelin enthusiasts to increase purchases of heavier-than-air aircraft, and fostered the development of the nascent German aircraft industry that by war's outset could produce more than 100 planes per month.[15]

Forget barnstormers and box kites; the German Army airplanes of 1914 had come a long way from the Wright Flyer.[16] Figure 39 shows two of the types most widely represented in first-line German service in August 1914.

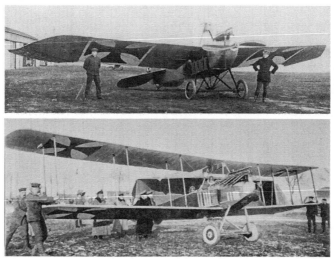

Figure 39. Reconnaissance aircraft: Rumpler Taube (top) and Albatros B.1 (bottom).

These weren't fighting aircraft—that took several more months—but they were effective for short-range reconnaissance. They and others like them weighed less than 2,500 lbs loaded with fuel for more than four hours and a two-man crew (an enlisted pilot and officer observer) and could cruise at more than 60 mph at an altitude of 4,000 ft. No radio was carried; reports had to wait until the plane returned from its mission.

At that height the horizon is 75 miles away, but the real range of visibility is usually much less, and the range at which distinct objects can be made out is less still. In reasonably good conditions it will normally be possible for a trained observer to see the signs of large-scale military activity to a distance of at least ten miles on either side of the airplane.

The Germans had about four first-line aircraft for every five miles of front in the west, so it should have been possible to keep the entire area ahead of the front under close and frequent surveillance out to a depth of at least 100 miles or more through the daylight hours. Since it took a week for approaching forces to march 100 miles this would have represented quite a good capability. Even if the enemy moved by rail it should have given at least a day's warning of approaching threats as the forces assembled and marched from the railhead.

Not universally, of course; sometimes the atmosphere didn't cooperate and in some places terrain or forest limited observation. But on the whole it should have been possible for commanders and staffs to form a reasonably good picture of what lay ahead of the front.

In fact even though considerable use was made of the aircraft, commanders frequently had little knowledge of what was going on around them. This was so even when the weather was favorable for flying and observation, as it generally was that August. The reason was poor organization, inadequate coordination and lack of a well-practiced doctrine for directing aerial reconnaissance operations.

The airplanes assigned to one command would be idle while other commands had too few to meet needs. Flights were sent to areas where the enemy was thought to be and not to those from which threats might emerge. Essential information was neglected because it conflicted with other reports or firmly-held preconceptions. Reports weren't forwarded to other headquarters because communications were poor or simply because no one thought to do it. Such problems weren't universal but they were common.

German commanders complained that they didn't have enough airplanes. But more airplanes would have done them only a little good without better organization, sound doctrine and more efficient operations. And with those things a great deal more could have been accomplished with the airplanes the Army had.

Because of the limits on airplane range the Supreme Army Headquarters was forced to rely on airships for long-range strategic reconnaissance, or try to. Exercises in peacetime had shown how fragile and vulnerable the Zeppelins and other airships were and little was expected of them. In fact they produced nothing at all.

Longer-range airplanes were possible with the technology of the time and some were soon produced, but nothing was done along those lines in Germany until too late for the crucial early phases of the war.[17] While twin-engined airplanes for broader reconnaissance would have been helpful, there really was no opening for developing them given the questionable state of the technology and the lack of enthusiasm from the War Ministry.

Telecommunications

BY EARLY SEPTEMBER 1914 THE crisis had been reached on the Western Front, especially on the German right wing. At 7:20PM on the 4th the Supreme Army Headquarters (by then located in Luxembourg City) radioed an urgent 60-word order to the field armies on the right wing. It was received by First Army at 7:15AM and at Second Army headquarters at 8:30AM, both on the 5th.[18]

Such a 12-plus hour delay wasn't at all unusual. In fact it was almost to be expected and 24-hour or longer delays were not rare. Together with comparable delays in the opposite direction it meant that Moltke was faced with the task of directing a fast-developing situation on the basis of information that would be more than 24 hours old before his orders in response to it were received.

It was out of the question. No one, no matter how brilliant and commanding, could conduct a campaign on that basis.

There were important reasons why Moltke couldn't simply go to the scene himself. He was also responsible for the center and left wings of the long German line, stretching 250 miles or so and for the actions in the east against Russia. Moreover he issued his orders on the Kaiser's authority and he couldn't drag the Kaiser with him.[19] In fact while he was busy other royal favorites were plotting to undermine him with the volatile monarch—especially the ambitious War Minister, General Erich von Falkenhayn, and the devious chief of the Kaiser's military cabinet, General Moriz von Lyncker.[20] The moment he showed any signs of faltering the two combined to shove him aside and replace him with Falkenhayn.

The expedient of putting First Army under the direction of the Second Army commander, Bülow, hadn't worked well. Bülow continued to view the situation from the Second Army perspective rather than that of the German forces as a whole and had treated First Army as an adjunct to his army.

Moltke's statements indicate that he had believed that doctrine would see his armies through, that on the basis of thousands of hours spent in exercises and war games the staff officers and commanders would all be thinking in harmony and know what to do to carry out the overall plan even when not in touch with the Supreme Army Headquarters. Spread over hundreds of miles as it was, he believed that the network of command would nevertheless be unified and synchronized by the force of doctrine.

The fundamental adequacy of the GGS operational doctrine and of the training of officers in how to apply it are important questions that will be taken up a bit later but here it's just important to recognize that doctrine proved not strong enough to bear the load of uniting and directing the operational maneuver of the seven field armies in the west. It was not self-evident in advance that this would be so but it's equally true that Moltke had no strong basis for assuming that it would be adequate.

Later in the war the Germans adopted (and improved upon) the Russian practice of establishing "army group" headquarters directing several field armies on behalf of Supreme Army Headquarters. But army groups couldn't be improvised.

It all came back to the fact that communications were essential—fast, reliable, secure, and flexible communications. What was available in that August and September fell far short of need or of what might reasonably have been provided with the resources at hand.

The electrical telegraph had revolutionized military communications in the mid–1800s, bringing a major increase in range, speed, and rate of communication. Generals had greeted it with mixed feelings, fearing that it would encourage distant superiors to meddle in their affairs, but there was no resisting it.

Reflecting on his experience in high command in the American Civil War, General William T. Sherman said of the telegraph,

> For the rapid transmission of orders in an army covering a large space of ground, the magnetic telegraph* is by far the best.... [T]he value of the magnetic telegraph in war cannot be exaggerated, as was illustrated by the perfect concert of action between the armies in Virginia and Georgia during 1864. Hardly a day intervened when General Grant did not know the exact state of facts with me, more than fifteen hundred miles away as the wires ran.[21]

By the end of the century, however, "modern communications" meant the telephone. The German style of command involved communicating objectives clearly and concisely and leaving the details to the field commander so the telephone suited it perfectly. Even the telegraph's grown-up offspring, the high-speed printing teletype, couldn't compete. In 1910 the German Army decided that the telephone would be its sole form of wired communication.[22]

The telephone of 1914 was different from the phones we know today. Today's telephone systems, whether cell, wireless or wired, are almost all electronic: they use active electronic components to amplify and clarify their signals making it possible to talk over any distance in normal conversational tones. Electronics also makes it possible to multiplex signals, sending many conversations or data streams over the same physical connection simultaneously.

---

*   "Magnetic telegraph" was then a term for what we know as the electric telegraph.

But the age of electronics was just dawning in 1914 and the first use of vacuum tubes for amplification in Germany didn't come until just after the initial campaigns. (Loading coils, non-electronic devices which improve signal clarity but offer no amplification, also were just on the verge of use.) Over normal telephone circuits, including all those used in the campaign, the power of the speaker's voice had to push enough electric current down the line to produce an audible signal at the other end. A speaker with a loud, clear voice—a parade-ground voice—could be heard more than 300 miles away over a good line.

Figure 40. German Army telephone linemen.

But a good line meant heavy wires, carefully strung and connected. Over light, quickly strung field wire even the most leather-lunged general was not going to be heard 30 miles away. Used for telegraph service a field line might work over distances of hundreds of miles but the army had committed to telephones which are much more demanding.

For communications beyond the reach of wires the Army had embraced one of the era's most dynamic technologies as a supplement, radio. Radio was only about 15 years old when war came but even in an extremely primitive state it was capable of remarkable things.

Figure 41. Strategic communications: 2kW radio sets.

When out of telephone contact, the field armies relied on heavy-duty Telefunken field radio sets mounted on horse-drawn carts like artillery caissons, transmitter on one cart and receiver on another as shown in Figure 41. The transmitter had an output of two kilowatts (2kW), powerful for its time. Normal operating frequency was about 300 kilohertz, low by today's standards. The transmitter cart also carried a one-cylinder four horsepower generator.

Although the set could be used for voice transmissions, intelligibility was quite poor at best and usable voice ranges didn't exceed a few dozen miles. For strategic communications radiotelegraphy was used. Supreme Army Headquarters had a truck-mounted radio station with somewhat more powerful equipment and could also transmit messages through powerful fixed transmitters in the fortresses at Cologne, Metz and Strassbourg.

In theory the 2kW horse-cart sets were supposed to be good for about 100 miles, while the fixed sets at the fortresses could reach to 600mi. In reality range varied a great deal with conditions. At night, at a time and place where interference was low, the signal might be clear 1,000 miles away. Daytime ranges were much shorter and any interference could cut effective range still more. A hot August with long days and lightning-filled thunderstorms (which can interfere even with very distant radios) plus many other active radio transmitters was very unfavorable and the situation was made worse because of unshielded vehicle and generator ignitions. As the distance between Moltke's headquarters and the right wing field armies stretched out to more than 150 miles messages frequently had to be relayed though intermediate stations.

To add to the problems the German cypher system had been chosen without considering the specific problems of radio communications. As a result a single burst of static affecting only a few letters could make an entire message unintelligible, requiring complete retransmission.

To do the work of communications the German Army had 25,000 signal troops led by 800 officers. In addition it had the support of the civil telecommunications agency with is resources of engineers and technicians.

All in all the signal resources the Army went to war with should have been adequate to assure reliable and fast communications among all of its major headquarters at essentially all times down to the corps level and often to the division level. We can say this with confidence because on the Eastern Front, where the conditions were in many ways more difficult, that was more or less what was accomplished.

The Western Front was another matter, as we've already seen at the start of this section. There was no particular communications planning or preparation for the campaign there; it was assumed that standard practices and procedures would be adequate. They weren't, not nearly. Communications troops and resources were distributed among the field army and corps headquarters with scarcely any central guidance or control.

It was part of the German Army tradition—and strength—to decentralize whatever it could. But communication was inevitably a matter of networks and could no more be fully decentralized than the railroads. What was needed was firm direction by officers who understood the technological demands and limitations as well as the military situation and needs. That's what was done for the railroad system supporting the campaign in the west where Groener was put in charge as Chief of Field Railways (*Chef des Feldeisenbahnwesens*). Though he held only a lieutenant-colonel's rank at that time he had years of experience in planning railroad operations to support military campaigns and knew everyone who played an important role. Many unexpected problems cropped up but under Groener's knowledgeable direction effective service was maintained.

The man appointed to direct communications for the Supreme Army Command (*Chef des Telegraphiewesens*) was an infantryman and General Staff officer, *Generalmajor* William Balck (1858–1924), with no special background for the job. He was noted as an expert on tactics but when he wrote a book on the tactical lessons of the war he had scarcely anything to say about communications. Whatever his virtues as a tactician he was not the man to conceive and execute an overall vision for communications. As a one-star general he had more weight to throw around than Groener but he lacked the experience to know where and how to use it.

Throughout the campaign communication between Moltke's headquarters and the field army headquarters on the right wing was far too spotty to allow him to exercise any effective overall direction. Communication among the field headquarters was often even more irregular. Yet at the same time there were always powerful communications resources that were going unutilized or underutilized. The experience in the East strongly suggests that better results would have been possible in the West with effective direction.

On the other side of the line Moltke's opposite number, Joffre, benefitted from France's excellent civil telephone and telegraph system. By keeping his headquarters close to the front he minimized the problems of distance. Moreover, the French used teletypes to transmit written information and orders and to relieve the telephones. Finally when telecommunications did not meet the need, Joffre had a powerful car driven by a Grand Prix champion to speed him to the subordinate headquarters where the action was hottest; he was seldom still. In Figure 42 we see him in a characteristic situation and pose, face-to-face with one of his commanders, leaving no doubt about the need—and the consequences of failing to meet it.

Figure 42. Joffre.

There are no comparable images of Moltke who as we've seen had reasons to keep his headquarters far to the rear and didn't visit the field armies. His uncle had recommended stationing a liaison officer from headquarters at each of the subordinate headquarters to assure that the supreme commander was kept fully aware of the situation and that his orders got through to the field army commander. The nephew sent officers out a few times during the campaign but did not maintain continuing liaison.

During the campaign *Oberstleutnant* Gerhard Tappen (1866–1943) headed the operations section at Supreme Army HQ and was Moltke's closest advisor. After the war, as a retired one-star general, Tappen said he thought that this was because there weren't enough well-qualified General Staff officers available.[23]

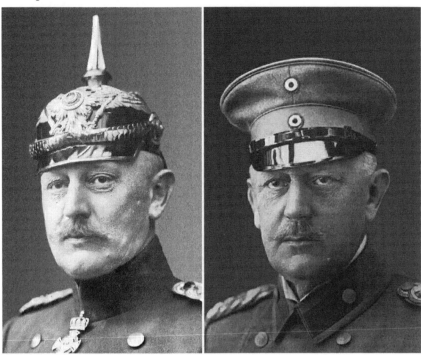

Figure 43. Moltke the Younger, 1906 and 1914.

The General Staff had hundreds of officers; there were too many as some saw it. In addition to the scores back in Berlin and at the Supreme Army Headquarters, every division had one, every corps a handful, every field army a dozen or so. At every level their function was fundamentally the same: to ensure that the mission of the formation was carried out as efficiently and effectively as possible according to General Staff doctrine. This could involve nudging the commander, or even giving him a strong shove, but the principal work of the General Staff officers was to organize and direct movement whether by rail, foot or by whatever means offered. It involved a great deal of work and was absolutely critical to mission accomplishment; the available officers were stretched thinly in doing it.

According to German ideas a General Staff officer who presented his views bluntly to his commander was not being insubordinate. It was part of the duties of his position and rank didn't enter into it. He could rely on the support not only of the Chief of Staff but the Kaiser himself.[24] In the same way a General Staff officer assigned to a field army as a liaison with the Supreme Army Headquarters could have asserted himself against efforts to keep him in the dark or control his reporting. Experienced senior staff officers close to Moltke would have been best but bright majors or captains would have been a huge improvement over none at all.

Shortage of qualified General Staff officers was a serious problem in many ways. While line officers might grumble and complain about staffs it was impossible to conduct war on a large scale without large and efficient staffs and equally impossible to make the staffs efficient without officers thoroughly trained in staff doctrine, thinking and functions.

But the failure to find the eight or ten officers it would have taken to keep liaison contacts at the headquarters of the field armies had especially serious consequences. The commanders were simply too deeply involved to be relied upon to provide dispassionately accurate reports of their situations, actions and accomplishments. Between August 20 and 24 for instance the army commanders in the west all painted pictures of great triumphs when they had really had achieved much less. At the same time the Eighth Army commander in East Prussia took excessive alarm at a fairly minor reversal. On the basis of the distorted picture Moltke issued some orders that made matters worse rather than better. It was no way to win a war.[25]

. . .

THE EXPLANATIONS FOR the failure of the German effort to knock France out of the war usually come down to Moltke's supposedly poor generalship and lack of sufficient troops.

The issues involved in adding troops have already been addressed in the context of the discussion of sweeping around Paris on page 110. But even if these could be resolved, it would remain true that more troops marching on foot with erratic direction from ill-informed commanders unable to coordinate their actions would have done little to improve the German Army's all-important ability to envelop and annihilate their enemies, rather than just shove them back.

To carry out the annihilation strategy taught by every General Staff chief from the elder Moltke to the younger, the commander needed to attack with strong forces on the enemy's flank. The out-flanking forces needed not just to hit the opponent from the side but to get deep enough to threaten his route of retreat and resupply. In the meantime the enemy had to stay where he was and not pull back away from the flank attack.

As we saw at page 86, at Mons the attackers were unable to find the Anglo-French flank for some hours. And before they could get around it, Sir John French, dull though he was, grew alarmed, disengaged his forces and retreated.

The Germans had hoped that if they simultaneously mounted a strong attack on the front it would "fix" the enemy forces in place and make it impossible for them to break contact and retreat while the flanking force was advancing. This had some validity in earlier wars fought at closer quarters where the disorder that was sure to accompany a retreat would open the defender to being immediately overrun. But in the conditions of 1914, with more dispersed forces, it proved possible for a hard-pressed force to escape in virtually every instance.[26]

So to actually envelop and annihilate an enemy force it was essential to have accurate and prompt information about where it was and to outflank it with a force that had a substantial advantage in mobility. And it all had to be coordinated promptly and precisely.

Even in ideal circumstances, even with excellent reconnaissance and communications as well as a highly mobile striking force, attempts at envelopment would often result in a retreat by at least a part of the opposing force rather than encirclement and annihilation. And when the retreat was begun as a deliberate choice by the French commander his forces would inevitably gain an initial lead; they could take measures to deceive and delay the pursuers who would need first to recognize what the real situation was and then re-form for the pursuit. Pursuers on foot could scarcely ever overtake a force retreating on foot except in especially favorable circumstances.[27]

The great Prussian General Staff theorist, Carl von Clausewitz (1780–1831), had long before analyzed the problems of pursuit and shown that the only real hope of annihilating a retreating enemy in most cases was through what he called "parallel pursuit" in which a separate column moving on a parallel road overtakes the retreating force and moves in to cut off the line of retreat or at least threaten it strongly enough to force the enemy to stand and fight.[28] In an earlier day, cavalry had sometimes been successful in parallel pursuit. But by 1914, mounted forces lacked the combat power needed to overcome infantry forces and survive in the face of their fire.

To make parallel pursuit possible it was essential to have accurate information about the retreating force as well as a speed advantage. In the wake of the Battle of Mons the German First Army was unable to catch the BEF not only because it wasn't fast enough but because its leaders had the wrong idea about the routes being taken by the British.

. . .

THE CRITICS OF Moltke's "generalship" seem clearly to be thinking of his ability to direct the operations of the field armies forcefully and decisively to meet the needs of the situation as it developed. But in 1914 he lacked the means to find out what the situation truly was or to communicate his directives, however forceful and decisive or otherwise they might have been.

Liaison officers in each army headquarters could have provided Moltke with a more dispassionate picture of the actual situation and ensured accurate and forceful transmission of his intentions to the field army commanders.

With better planning and preparation, thorough advance testing and exercising, and a strong, knowledgeable officer in charge of communications, the high command could have kept in close touch with the field army headquarters, and the headquarters with one another.

And in a similar way, with good organization, thorough training, sound doctrine and strong direction the airplane reconnaissance force could have produced a substantially more comprehensive picture of the situation up to 100 miles ahead of the German forces. With a reliable and well-organized communications net the headquarters liaison officers could have ensured that the information was shared with Moltke's headquarters as well as the commanders of other formations.

Finally with large yet still affordable investments (investments that would have yielded important benefits for the economy) and intensive development of tactics and doctrine Moltke could have had a motorized force of two corps with a great mobility advantage over enemies who were limited to moving afoot.

Taken together these innovations in reconnaissance and communications could have provided Moltke (and his field army commanders) with timely knowledge of opportunities and threats all along the German front. And a truck-mobile striking force could have provided the means to take early and decisive advantage of the knowledge. These innovations could have made it at least fairly possible for the Moltke/Schlieffen plans to succeed without the need for extraordinary good luck. And no amount of genius or "will" could make up for their lack.

Of course if the French and British had learned of a German initiative to build motorized forces—as they very probably would have—they could have developed their own motorized formations, especially as France's motor vehicle industry was stronger than Germany's. And even without them the Allies might have been able to avoid defeat. If it was not to take very great risks, risks that threatened its existence, the German Empire needed more than technology and organization alone could provide.

x. Delusions of Strategy

B Y MID-SEPTEMBER GERMANY'S STRATEGY in the west had been decisively defeated. In part it had been defeated by the French with some help from the Belgians and British. And in great part it had been defeated by time, distance, and failures of imagination, foresight and preparation. As it turned out it was a defeat Germany would spend more than four years, much of her young manhood and virtually all of her economic strength trying to reverse—and ultimately fail.

It's possible that the German Army might have overcome its obstacles in September 1914 and defeated the Allies given more luck on top of that it had already enjoyed. It would have been even more possible given better imagination, foresight and preparation—possible, but far from certain, not even tremendously likely. Yet Germany's leaders had chosen to play *va banque*, to stake the future of the Empire on the success of the Schlieffen Plan, or Moltke Plan, or whatever one elects to call it.

Wars are hard to stop even when it becomes clear that there's been an awful mistake. Unless one side were completely conquered and subjugated peace in Europe would require some measure of trust—and the German plan and the way it was executed made it very hard for anyone to trust the Imperial government.

The invasion of neutral Luxembourg was seen as cynical; that of neutral Belgium as a barbaric moral outrage, a brutal rejection of the mores that bound Europeans in a common civilization. First there was the arrogance of the German presumption that they had a right to invade because it suited their plans to do so and moreover that in deciding to oppose them and defend their homeland the Belgians had forfeited all rights.

Then in what's hard to see as anything but a systematic terror campaign intended to demoralize the Belgians and speed their conquest, the invading troops murdered nearly 6,000 unarmed civilians out of hand, used civilians as "human shields" in combat, looted and burned 25,000 homes and buildings, and destroyed or desecrated ancient cultural monuments. The Germans and their apologists claimed excuses of snipers, guerillas, and Belgian atrocities (!). But most Europeans looked with horror and revulsion and so did most Americans. They were well aware that war was a dirty business at best but it hadn't been waged on such terms in Northwestern Europe since the mid–1600s.[1]

By German lights the situation had been made very clear and fully justified in the 12-hour ultimatum delivered to the Belgians at 7PM on August 2. Germany was acting in "self-protection" and the Belgians should be happy to extend the hand of friendship in welcome. But should the Belgians somehow insist on defending their sovereignty and neutrality then Germany could "undertake no obligations towards Belgium, but the eventual adjustment of the relations between the two States must be left to the decision of arms."[2]

In other words as a matter of "military necessity" the Belgians had been made "an offer you can't refuse," and since they had refused it the Germans washed their hands of all responsibility. A terror campaign against Belgium's civilian population was simply a logical measure to assure success. There's no evidence that anyone at high levels actually declared such a policy but the Germans never provided another explanation. They continued to deny the truth of what their officers were doing in Belgium which heightened suspicions. It was natural and inevitable—and not clearly wrong—for the Allies to suspect that it was a calculated and cynical campaign and thus to conclude that the German Empire was a wholly amoral and cynical state that could never be trusted.[3]

All in all the invasion of Belgium and the conduct of the invaders was an announcement that this was to be total war, war to the knife, war without compromise or settlement short of total victory or absolute defeat. Frederick the Great could lose one of his wars and survive, as sometimes he did. But in the name of the last ruler of Frederick's line his Great General Staff cast that option to the winds. In November 1918 the Allies demanded regime change as the price of peace for an exhausted Germany haunted by famine.

. . .

MOREOVER, THE VIOLATION of Belgium was a primary factor in ensuring ultimate German defeat. This was because it ensured Britain intervention on the side of France and Russia. Without a British blockade Germany would have been able to carry on enough foreign trade to sustain the food supply and industrial production. In a protracted conflict there was a good chance that the German Army could fight the Russian and French armies to a stalemate in which Britain would come to feel impelled to pressure both sides to a compromise settlement. This would have preserved the German Empire and very likely have brought it some gains.

With Britain in the war its Royal Navy grew to become the Empire's most deadly adversary. Its ruthless blockade faced Germany with industrial collapse, severe privation, and ultimately starvation. At the same time not only Britain's sea power but her political and financial connections ensured that the Allies could draw freely on the resources of the world's greatest industrial and agricultural power, the United States. In the attempt to break the blockade, cut off the flow of American goods, and force Britain from the war the Kaiser's regime resorted to increasingly reckless and ill-conceived measures that ultimately brought the United States to the Allied side.

In a remarkably short time (with a good deal of British and French help) the Americans built up a large army that was good enough to play a serious part in the closing months of the war, making swift German defeat absolutely certain.

. . .

SO THE GERMAN PLAN with its sweep through Belgium led to the destruction of the Empire. Surely that wasn't Schlieffen's and Moltke's purpose, but what was?

For many years most historians presented the Schlieffen Plan—by which they meant the plan that had guided Germany's armies in August and early September of 1914—as a recipe for aggression and conquest. Often they pointed to Prussia's history over the preceding three centuries. In the early 1600s the Hohenzollerns—the Kaiser's family—had been masters only of a few scattered, poor territories in Germany and Poland, just a handful out of hundreds of statelets incorporated into the Austrian-ruled Holy Roman Empire and the Kingdom of Poland. (The first Hohenzollern to claim the dignity of kingship was Frederick the Great's grandfather, who took the title in 1701, naming his territories after the easternmost province, Prussia.)

By relentless expansion the Hohenzollerns had come by 1871 to rule over the newly-consolidated German Empire. Surely, many insist, 1914 could only have been intended to mark the next step in the long history of Hohenzollern aggression and expansion.

Yet most of the expansion had come through making love—and deals—rather than war. The Hohenzollerns had a knack for marrying well and making sharp property deals. No doubt it was possible to make better deals with a great army in the wings but in fact the Prussian/German armies were only great in the time of Frederick the Great and after 1860. Objectively the Hohenzollerns were certainly no more aggressive or expansionistic than Russia's Romanovs, Austria's Habsburgs or the various Italian and French regimes. If their results seemed more impressive it was at least partly because in Germany they were expanding to fill what was essentially a political vacuum.

To a very large extent, Prussian/German expansion was driven by anxieties about security. The Prussian concern about vulnerability and defense and the focus on active defense dated from the first half of the 1600s, the days of the Thirty Years War, when the statelets that were to become Prussia were small, weak and caught up in a Great-Power war. For three decades the greatest armies in Europe ranged across Germany waging war with demonic savagery and neither Prussia nor most of the other German states had the power to offer any effective resistance. The population of Germany was reduced by as much as 30 percent by the war and its side effects and the survivors were indelibly scarred.[4]

"Never again!" was the European response. If Europeans were bound to make war upon one another, as they took to be inevitable, then war and the states that made it had to be subject to some sort of limits. The horrors of the war and other conflicts of the time stimulated legal and moral philosophers (most notably Hugo Grotius) to update the Medieval law of war to square with Christian belief and humanistic ethics as well as the realities of the international political order, and monarchs all over Western Europe supported it at least in principle.

The Prussians had suffered terribly in the Thirty Years War and to them, "Never again!" meant something different. It was the state's responsibility to protect itself from such calamities and the duty of every subject to do whatever this required of him. Self-preservation was the supreme law and there could be no compromise.

Prussia never had the luxury of defensible borders. Her territories sat out on the North German Plain exposed from all sides. Her soldiers early concluded that a good offense was the *only* defense in their situation. Regardless of whether the nation's strategic objectives in the conflict were expansionary or conservative the enemy forces had to be met and promptly and decisively defeated, preferably beyond Prussia's borders. Prussia's terms for peace might be moderate (and usually were) but she depended on military victories to provide negotiating leverage.

Prussia might face threats on several different borders. Her statesmen attempted to ensure that only one enemy really threatened at any one time, as Bismarck did so successfully, but when that failed her soldiers exploited her central position to operate on interior lines. That is they shifted forces swiftly from one front to another across Prussian territory as need demanded or opportunity offered. If they were used well the advantages of interior lines could balance out some of the vulnerabilities of the nation's exposed position.[5] That was a key reason why Prussian leaders took a strong early interest in railways.

As discussed earlier (page 64) Germany had no motives for conquest: there simply was no territory that her leaders wanted. But if war came, for whatever reason, the military leadership wanted to defeat their enemies so the nation's leaders could dictate whatever terms seemed desirable.

. . .

GIVEN GERMANY'S LACK of territorial ambitions it seemed reasonable to assume that it would be the French who would attack Germany rather than the other way around. In particular, they might thrust into Alsace-Lorraine in an effort to recapture the lost provinces. Or perhaps the Russians would attack in the east. In either case the German defenders could wait in their lair like a bear feigning sleep until the attacker had fully committed himself and advanced well within reach. Then with a swift rake of his claws the bear could catch, rend, and crush him. While the defeated attacker was struggling to recover the bear could swiftly hop a train to repeat the process with another threat.

The elder Moltke had pointed out the strength of such an offensive-defensive strategy decades earlier and Schlieffen often played scenarios like this in his exercises and war games. As time went on, he increasingly used the rails not only to shift forces between theaters but to outmaneuver and outrun the enemy.[6]

But what if Germany gave a war and nobody came? What if Germany saw some reason for war but France and Russia had no reason to attack her? The Chief of the General Staff couldn't very well tell the Kaiser or Chancellor, "Sorry boss, we can't win until they attack," could he?

In the early 1900s Germany's leaders fecklessly involved her in meaningless quarrels with France and Britain over what were essentially symbolic colonial matters. The economic issues were trivial and there were no strategic issues but some people in high places were eager to launch what would have amounted to little more than history's worst meaningless bar brawl over them. The Kaiser played his usual irresponsible and unhelpful role, but he did hold back from war in the end.

Together with the turmoil in the Balkans this fed German fears of "encirclement," of an "iron ring" of hostile powers gathering around her. To a great extent it was "self-encirclement," generated in response to perceptions of unrestrained German aggressiveness.[7]

Perhaps it was this that led Schlieffen to experiment with scenarios in which it was his forces rather than the French who led off with an offensive, an offensive to "break the iron ring," as hyper-patriotic German politicians and newspaper editors so often put it.

Three years or so after he retired, Schlieffen wrote an essay that was later published under the title "War Today."[8] Much of it concerns matters of tactics, operations, and technology, but it closes with a dark and profoundly distorted strategic vision. "Peaceable" Germany is surrounded, he warns, encircled by enemies on all sides. Even though she "was free of any desire for conquest," she is threatened by her "vengeful hidden enemy," France, which only waits the moment to strike. "The powerful expansion of Germany's industry and trade has earned her another implacable enemy—Britain." And "the inherited antipathy of the Slavs towards the Germans" has made Russia too into an enemy to be feared. An "iron ring" has been thrown around Germany as all the states on her borders have armed against her, even those that were supposedly neutral. And there is a good deal more in this vein. Only if Germany remains resolute and united, along with Austria-Hungary, and builds up her Army can she face down her craven and weak-willed assailants and secure the peace.[9] Before publishing this Schlieffen had circulated it widely among senior officers and officials, suggesting that this virtually unhinged fantasy reflected his real views. And the absence of criticism suggests that they were widely shared.[10]

Schlieffen had been asked by the editors to write on how peace might be preserved, which may be why he allowed that this "immense" danger "diminishes somewhat when one examines it more closely." Or this may have been his real view—we cannot be sure.

Perhaps it was his apocalyptic vision of encirclement by shadowy enemies that led Schlieffen after 1900 to experiment with scenarios in which it was his forces rather than the French who led off with an offensive, an offensive to "break the iron ring," as hyper-patriotic German politicians and newspaper editors so often put it.

All involved variations on the "Schlieffen Plan" theme of a wide sweep by the German right wing through Belgium in order to out-flank the French on their left. Rather than wait in his lair the Ger-man bear would lunge to the right, sweeping up his enemy in his right paw. (A thrust on the left was unattractive because breaching the French belt of fortifications stretching from Belfort to Verdun (as seen in Figure 20) would be a slow and costly process.*)

These scenarios never went for very long. The Germans who were playing the French side advanced to meet the bear in Belgium or tried to outflank him in turn on his left. Sometimes they won but usually the bear got his prey. The action never reached the vicinity of Paris, and the Russians were always a factor.

Perhaps Schlieffen wondered what would happen if the French played more cautiously, falling back to avoid being swept up. In his 1906 memorandum he observes that the German attack would lose force as it advanced and that the French might very well be able to hold on a line stretching between the great fortresses of Paris and Verdun via La Fère or perhaps Rheims.

Could the bear reach all the way around Paris and envelop the French right flank in a case like this? The 1906 think piece memo-randum explores this issue and seems to say that it might work but only with a substantially bigger bear having a much wider reach. Zuber has suggested that this represented a call for a great expansion of the Army but it seems at least equally plausible to read it as a warning about the problems, costs and risks of an offensive strategy rather than the counteroffensive one that his exercises and war games suggest Schlieffen preferred. Maybe it really was a subtle way of warning, "Sorry boss, we can't win until they attack." In 1914, in any event, Moltke proved the point: he tried to pursue an offensive strategy without a major numerical edge (actually with a numerical deficit) and could not make it work. Oddly, as Zuber has shown the

---

*   The apparent gap between Nancy and Èpinal was an illusion, or perhaps a trap, with natural defenses so strong as not to need permanent fortification.

overall pattern of Moltke's staff rides and war games resembled those played by Schlieffen rather than the "Schlieffen Plan" 1906 think piece.

Why in 1914 did Moltke feel called upon to gamble everything on what he had every reason to believe was a risky strategy, a strategy he presumably knew (if only from reading Schlieffen's memo) could end up requiring more troops than he had? It was certainly a considered decision; while the course of operations was deliberately kept fluid the initial deployments were of necessity fixed long in advance and could not be changed quickly.

As part of his effort to supply Chancellor Bethmann Hollweg with arguments to support an Army increase, 18 months before the war, Moltke told him

> Germany's central position will compel her to ... hold one front defensively with comparatively weak forces in order to be able to take the offensive on the ... French [front]. A speedy decision may be hoped for on that side, while an offensive against Russia would be an interminable affair. But if we are to take the offensive against France, it would be necessary to violate the neutrality of Belgium. It is only by an advance across Belgian territory that we can hope to attack and defeat the French army in the open field. On this route we shall meet the English Expeditionary Force and— unless we succeed in coming to some arrangement with Belgium—the Belgian army also. At the same time, this operation is more promising than a frontal attack on the French fortified eastern frontier.[11]

There seems no obvious reason to doubt Moltke's candor here; it's consistent with what he said to his staff in exercise critiques and probably represents his personal views. Thus he expected the bear to run at top speed through Belgium so he could catch the French in the open and defeat them thoroughly before dashing to the east in time to deal with the oncoming Russians. At best it was a great deal of sprinting. It takes the breath away just to think about it.

Wars are filled with chance. It was not altogether impossible that the iron dice could have fallen in Germany's favor with France quitting the war after sharp initial defeats and freeing the bulk of German forces to swing to the east. But war's surprises are much more frequently unpleasant; usually both sides are repeatedly and bitterly disappointed.

If the French put up much opposition and refused to give up easily then it was bound to take a very minimum of 45 days to inflict serious defeat on them. If forces were then pulled away to reinforce the Eastern Front they'd begin to get there around day 60.

It was possible, of course, that the French would give up after a serious defeat that annihilated much of their army. But in 1870, after superior German forces had annihilated virtually all of the French Army in 45 days, eight months of additional fighting was needed to get the French leaders to the peace table. Germany in 1914 did not enjoy the numerical advantage she had held in 1870 and France no longer suffered such deep internal divisions or feckless leadership. Moltke was widely known for his pessimistic character so it's hard to imagine that he counted on a quick surrender. More likely he hoped to inflict enough damage to keep the French on the defensive for a few months while he dealt with the Russians.

We certainly can give him credit for audacity. The question is how much credit audacity merits in such a case.

. . .

BELGIUM IN 1914 was in much the same position that Prussia had been in during the Thirty Years War, but the officers who plotted her violation and destruction saw themselves as following their highest and noblest duty, and those who led their troops across Belgium's territory felt the same way.

Belgium had to be subjugated immediately and completely; it was essential to Germany and therefore no scruples could stand in the way. As Moltke later wrote to his wife,

> What rivers of blood have already flowed, what nameless sorrow has come over the countless innocents whose houses have been burnt and pillaged! I am often overcome by dread when I think of this and I feel I should take responsibility for this horror; and yet, I could not have acted otherwise than I did.[12]

Similar expressions can be found in the letters and diaries of many other officers, the sentiments not of inhuman monsters but of quite ordinary humans prompted to monstrous acts by their conception of duty.

Schlieffen, Moltke, and the other top planners were aware that some at least would question the legitimacy of invading Belgium. (No one seems to have felt much concern about the invasion of Luxembourg.) But only the "enemies" of Germany would make any real fuss they believed; others would understand Germany's military necessity. And success would forgive all they confidently proclaimed. The Kaiser seemed more than content with this, at least when the Moon was full. The civilian leadership went along, with greater or lesser misgivings.

One issue raised by the civilians was the response of Britain. Some predicted that respecting Belgian neutrality would keep Britain out of the war, while invading Belgium would assure British intervention.[*] But the military leaders scoffed. The "English," as they always referred to them, were implacably hostile and anyway their army was too small to count for anything whatever. Success would right all wrongs they reiterated and only free use of the Belgian corridor would assure swift success.

· · ·

IT WAS CONFIDENCE in the Army and its plans above all that emboldened Germany's leaders to go to war in 1914. But it was confidence that was to be mocked by events.

Could it have been in the power of the Great General Staff to cast plans more worthy of confidence? Given that Germany's leaders felt compelled to back the Dual Monarchy in the face of Russian determination could any plans have given better assurance?

Actually, the narrowness of the Franco-German frontier could have been seen as a benefit rather than an obstacle. Not only was it narrow, but on the German side it was clogged with unwelcoming terrain and fortified cities. There were semi-open corridors for invasion but no broad front. None of the corridors could accept more than a fraction of the French forces and all offered good opportunities for counterattacks. Even if opposed only by modest German forces, any invasion directly into Germany was bound to be slow and risky.

---

[*]   In hindsight it appears that this was quite accurate.

Much the same was true on the Eastern Front, where the Russians were forced to neutralize the long eastward-lapping tongue of East Prussia before they could safely push west. Again, any invasion of East Prussia had to proceed in corridors, raising the prospect that a defending army could defeat one force and then scoot over by rail to do the same against the next. In fact this had been pointed out by Schlieffen in 1894 and it's exactly what the single German field army in the east did twenty years later to annihilate much larger Russian forces in what's known as the Battle of Tannenberg.

So far as defending Germany went in 1914 the GGS could have placed moderate defense forces in Alsace-Lorraine opposite France and in East Prussia opposite Russia and had a substantial swing force that could be shifted by rail to wherever the best opportunity for decisive counterattack could be found.

Moltke was very familiar with such strategies and their advantages; he had played variants in many exercises and war games. His reluctance to rely on a defensive-offensive approach in 1914 seems to have stemmed from two principal concerns. First, he feared that if he did not force the pace the French and Russians might both refrain from attacking until the Russians had built overwhelming forces in the east. Second, he believed that Germany's economy would break down after a year of being cut off from imported raw materials. An added concern was uncertainty about the effect of a long period of inaction on the fighting efficiency and spirit of the German Army.

Talleyrand, Napoléon's foreign minister, had cautioned his master that it was possible to do anything with bayonets except sit on them. It was an admonition that in 1914 would have applied more strongly to the French and Russians than to the Germans. Defensive alliances are difficult to hold together except in the face of an immediate common threat. The Franco-Russian alliance was especially problematic because of the tremendous political differences between the two and because they would be fighting hundreds of miles from one another rather than shoulder to shoulder. In an effort to bridge their mutual suspicions they had agreed to attack Germany simultaneously, essentially as soon as France had fully mobilized her forces (and at a point where Russia had only partly mobilized hers).

Any major French delay in operations against Germany in the West would have faced Russia with a serious dilemma. Because her whole rationale for war was to protect Serbia from Austria-Hungary's retaliation for Sarajevo she needed to attack the Dual Monarchy before it could do serious damage to her Serbian client. But the Germans could fall upon the rear of any forces committed against the Habsburg lands unless they were neutralized by a spoiling attack on East Prussia. Thus an offensive against the German Eastern Front could not be delayed a great deal without risking compromise to Russia's fundamental war aim. This meant that the Russians had to persuade the French to attack promptly in the West so that they did not end up facing the entire combined German and Austro-Hungarian strength.

The economic concerns were real, but they were less dire than Moltke seems to have imagined and some preparation could have ameliorated them substantially. Moreover they would also have weighed heavily on Russia and France, in some ways more than on Germany. The economic problems would have been more serious for Germany's ally, Austria-Hungary, than for Germany herself.[13]

Any issues of army morale would probably have been less troublesome for Germany than for her foes.

It all was as calculable as anything in war ever is. The German bear had every reason for confidence that if he waited in his lair his enemies would put themselves in his reach in good time.

Once combat was joined the Germans had confidence in the ability of their troops to win even against odds due to their sound doctrine, excellent training and high-quality armament and equipment. They had reasons for confidence based on what they had been able to learn of their opponents' armies and it proved to be amply justified. To translate these superiorities into decisive victories the Germans would also need the capabilities in reconnaissance, communications, and mobility outlined in the preceding chapter. Without them they would have found themselves usually unable to close the trap at these smaller scales just as they did at large scale in the "Schlieffen Plan" campaign of 1914.

Another essential was better preparation of the German economy. The fighting forces depended a great deal on industry for production of ammunition, weapons and war matériel of all kinds, yet they drafted many of the skilled workers industry needed and sent them off to carry rifles, seriously disrupting production. And industry depended on imported inputs which were cut off by the British blockade, especially for ammunition manufacture.

Agriculture too depended on imports particularly for fertilizer and couldn't produce enough food to meet nutritional needs without them.

Management of manpower resources, stockpiles of critical raw materials and development of import substitutes were all recognized before the war as essential to maintaining military strength. There were articles, memoranda and conferences but essentially no action. The problem again was the fragmented structure of authority in the German government which permitted and actually encouraged resistance to such initiatives. Unless the problem got attention at the highest levels there was no prospect of real action.[14]

. . .

OF COURSE THE GERMANS could never have inflicted outright military defeat on either France or Russia by active defense. But how much value would there have been in an outright victory? And regardless of value, what could an offensive have achieved that active defense could not?

In 1871 Germany had won victory over France. This had brought it two doubtful prizes: territory that was a permanent obstacle to ever making a real settlement with France and a large monetary indemnity that upset the German economy. In 1914 territorial acquisitions and monetary indemnities would have been at least equivalently problematic, and certainly not worth the price, whether in human or economic terms.

In any event, it was not for territory or gold that Germany went to war. She could defeat the threat to Austria-Hungary and improve her own security position much more surely and at far lower cost with a strategy of active defense.

With heavy casualties but without victories and without the threat of German invasion, support for the war would have dissipated sooner rather than later in both France and Russia. If the German government had proclaimed at the outset that it was only fighting in defense of itself and its ally and had no other war aims it would have been in a strong position to make peace with the humiliated and exhausted French and Russians on a basis of *status quo ante*. It's all but certain that the French government would have fallen and if revolution had not toppled the Czar it is clear that his regime would be seriously compromised. It's very hard to see how the French and Russians could ever have reassembled their alliance. Germany would pay substantial costs but could have emerged in a strengthened position while taking much less risk.

One of the risks that the Germans would have had an excellent chance of avoiding would be war with Britain. While Grey and his allies who led their country into war had some objectives that were independent of Belgium the German invasion of Belgium, with the certainty that it was to be followed by large-scale invasion of France, was the key to gaining broad enough support both in the Cabinet and Parliament to make intervention possible. There could scarcely have been a way to generate wide enthusiasm for joining France in invading Germany in order to prevent Germany from preventing Russia from invading Austria-Hungary to prevent her from visiting retribution on Serbia, regardless of what the clever men at the head of His Majesty's Government might have thought about the grand geopolitics of the issue.

Of course it was Germany's need to protect Austria-Hungary that was the problem. It's often contended that Austria-Hungary was sure to collapse in any event but that's wisdom after the fact. At the time she was widely seen as viable and even vibrant. There was no inevitability to her destruction.[15]

Unfortunately for Austria-Hungary however her army was weak and especially ill-led. The Army's budget and manpower authorizations were caught up in political bickering in and between the country's two parliaments.* As a result the Army was smaller than it needed to be or could readily have been and the troops were inadequately trained and equipped.

Nevertheless the Army was well disciplined and cohesive and might have done reasonably well if it hadn't been so miserably led from the top, particularly by the chief of staff, *General der Infanterie* Franz Freiherr Conrad von Hötzendorf† (1852–1925). He was well regarded at the time but it's hard to imagine why.

The Germans felt that if Austria-Hungary was threatened they had to respond not only because of their treaty but because they couldn't afford to lose their last significant ally. (It's questionable in the larger scheme of things how necessary it truly was for Germany to preserve the Dual Monarchy, but that's another issue.) And the top leaders in Austria-Hungary, at least on the Austrian side, were well aware that they needed Germany.

This ought to have led to close cooperation on planning and preparations but never did, or at least not until the war was already going catastrophically for the Dual Monarchy. The pattern was set by Bismarck, who made the link in 1879 but wanted to avoid encouraging any Habsburg adventurism. So the alliance was a skeleton without flesh and largely remained so until the final half decade before the war. Even then cooperation was far too limited to do real good.[16]

Moltke's obsession was that Germany's security demanded military defeat of France, while Conrad's was that Austria-Hungary's demanded defeat of Serbia. Both turned their backs on Russia. And because neither had been forthright, each country depended on the other to defend her from Russia. The Germans acting cautiously and with geography on their side decisively turned back the threat to East Prussia. But the Austro-Hungarians moving rashly out from the shelter of the Carpathian Mountains onto the open northeastern plains suffered crippling defeat. They never really recovered.

In 1914 Germany and Austria-Hungary pursued a strategy that offered what seemed like glittering payoffs: the complete defeat and

---

*   One for the Austrian half and the other for the Hungarian.
†   Conrad von Hötzendorf was his compound surname. Usually referred to simply as Conrad.

neutralization of their opponents for a very long time to come. But it involved extraordinary risks.

With realistic planning and coordination it would have been possible for both partners to have an effective defense that would make both French and Russian assaults unproductive and very costly—too costly to be continued indefinitely. This would also permit the partners to punish Serbia appropriately for her very real and serious sins, if not as quickly or completely as Conrad wished. It would have given them a very good chance of achieving a peace which would leave their would-be invaders chastened, weakened and disarrayed enough to impose a stable security regime in Europe for some years. And at worst it would have permitted them to avoid the overthrow of their regimes and wholesale loss of territory.

XI. What Were They *Thinking?*

IN PLANNING AND PREPARATIONS IN the years preceding 1914, Germany passed over options for improving her military capabilities through better reconnaissance and intelligence, command and control, and motorization. While there were various agencies and officers who might have taken these options up, the natural focus would have been the Great General Staff.

It's possible that serious investigation would have revealed crippling problems with these options that haven't emerged here. But they were not turned down following deep probing; instead they were never weighed at all. They were simply too outlandish even to be thought about by the world's premier planning organization.

At the same time the GGS committed Germany to pursuing total victory regardless of risk. Strategies of potentially lower risk were mentioned but rejected out of hand without real analysis.

What were they *thinking?* Was some Freudian death urge at work here? Wagnerian blind fate?

Perhaps. But modern knowledge of how humans make decisions permits us to explain their thinking in much more circumstantial terms, in terms of processes that can be seen at work in psychological experiments and in the world all around us; processes we can see at work within ourselves if we're willing to look.

A later book in this series will take up the question of decision and its problems in more depth and generality[1], but some brief consideration of the specifics here will round out our story in important ways.

. . .

THE GENERAL STAFF was one of the very most important institutions of the Imperial German government. By 1914 its power and prestige had been growing steadily for nearly a century. It occupied the central control position in the security apparatus of a nation for which security was a central concern. In times of greatest stress its chief exercised the authority of the sovereign. No one had the knowledge and authority to challenge its decisions, and on them rested the fate of the German Empire.

For almost all of its officers, service in the General Staff meant membership in a social group at the very center of the affairs of their state. Entry was by a process of selection, training, internship, examination, and initiation demanding the very greatest intellectual exertions and highest dedication, extending over many years. It was like nothing so much as a military monastic order of crusader knights. In a country where a great many men wore uniform all the time, where the monarch himself was scarcely ever seen out of uniform, the distinctive insignia of the General Staff officer conveyed high prestige. Even a mid-grade officer in the General Staff, even a major or a captain, might be entrusted with responsibilities of the most crucial kind. In scarcely any other group that was open to the talents could a man rise so high, or feel so exalted.

The top leaders of the Great General Staff, at the pinnacle of the General Staff as a whole, strove constantly to cultivate critical thought and forthright expression among all the officers of the Staff. Officers were frequently presented with problems to test their thinking and knowledge and always reminded that there were no set solutions.

That there were expectations and standards, however, was evident to all. The objective was to instill the wisdom of the senior officers in the juniors while also fostering their own initiative and insight. Some solutions to problems brought an officer more credit than others, and an officer whose work failed to gain high enough marks might be relegated to lesser assignments, face poorer promotion prospects or even be sent down. The centrality of the group in the lives of its members gave these sanctions tremendous power. Not only the officer's career success but much of his own conception of self-worth was sure to ride on his place in the General Staff as a group.

Thus no matter how strong and sincere its leadership's support for a culture of intellectual openness and iconoclasm, General Staff officers were also bound to feel strong pressures toward conformity. The balance between the two varied from issue to issue and officer to officer.

. . .

THERE'S LITTLE INFORMATION about the inner workings of the Great General Staff in the years before the First World War but we get some impressions.

Hermann Thomsen (1867–1942) was a combat engineer (*Pionier*) officer who attended the War Academy and joined the GGS in 1905 as a captain (*Hauptmann*).[*] He was assigned to the Engineer and Fortress Department which among its other duties dealt with technology in general.[2]

This was the period of greatest excitement about Zeppelins but Thomsen became an early doubter and by 1907 was pointing to the new technology of airplanes where the French held a wide lead over Germany. At the end of the year he was made head of a GGS section responsible for aviation, motor vehicles and telecommunications, a post he held for more than six years. This was the period of the truck subsidy program, the excitement and disappointment with the Zeppelins, building an airplane fleet, the full changeover from telegraph to telephone and the introduction of radio as an important means of

---

[*]   Promoted to major 1911. Also referred to as von der Lieth-Thomsen—in this case simply a place name not denoting nobility.

communication, so we may feel sure that Thomsen was a pretty busy junior section chief.

For much of this Thomsen reported to Erich Ludendorff, then a lieutenant colonel (full colonel from 1911) and operations department head. Ludendorff was brilliant, obsessive, and extraordinarily intense, and a strong supporter of military aviation and of Thomsen. He made powerful enemies in the course of his crusades to strengthen the Army and was rusticated to a regimental command early in 1913. Thomsen remained in place for another year before going to a railway regiment as its staff officer. The coming of war changed the fortunes of both very dramatically.

Given all the things he was responsible for it would be understandable if Thomsen perhaps did not think of ideas like motorizing infantry, or see it as urgent to do battle with the War Ministry over better organization for aerial reconnaissance and strategic communications. During the war to come he played a central part in organizing the German Army Air Force (*Luftstreitkräfte*) and in the 1920s and 1930s had an important role in developing the independent national air arm or *Luftwaffe*.[3] But he is not credited with having a major part in developing concepts for employing aircraft in war; that is usually assigned to others. Perhaps he simply did not tend to think along such lines.

Figure 44. Thomsen about 1917–18 (left) and
Ludendorff about 1914–16 (right).

On an issue such as motorization that didn't touch the leader-ship's central concerns it seems likely that any officer who took an interest and made proposals would get a fair hearing even if it was not within his official range of responsibilities, and that traces of the discussion would have appeared in the professional military press that flourished in that era. We can feel pretty sure that either it didn't occur to anyone, or that anyone it did occur to declined to raise an issue that was bound to be contentious in the Army as a whole. More or less the same is true of command and control ar-rangements and those for reconnaissance and intelligence.

. . .

QUESTIONS OF FUNDAMENTAL national and military strategy by con-trast were very central and would have been addressed within the core GGS group. There was discussion of them in the press, some contributed by officers, but it would have been only the most rash of GGS officers from outside the core group who would have pressed his views.

Within the core leadership the chief of the GGS carried the greatest weight but he needed the support or at least acquiescence of the others. Moreover, for policies at this level the GGS had to have the agreement of others outside the GGS, including the Kaiser and his immediate circle as well as the Prussian Minister of War, the Chancellor, and the core leadership of the Foreign Ministry. The GGS chief was the link among these and had to mediate any shift in the policy consensus.[4]

It would have been open to the Kaiser or the Chancellor to initi-ate a discussion on top-level national policy and advance proposals for change. But Wilhelm II was too erratic and unfocused himself and took care to ensure that the Chancellor was not a strong person-ality and lacked the tools to build a strong base of power. Except in Bismarck's reign the military had played the leading role in such de-cisions for a century and more. Wilhelm derived much of his sense of who he was from his identification with the military and had no desire to see the military's power diminished. He lacked the imagi-nation and foresight to recognize the terrible danger this posed to his throne and dynasty.

It would also have been open to Moltke to have considered whether the rewards of military victory against France and Russia were so transcendent as to fully justify the immense risks it entailed. Intellectually Moltke's remarks show that he recognized he was wagering the whole fate of the Empire. And he also recognized that after even the most thoroughgoing defeat of their armies the path to preventing France and Russia—to say nothing of Britain—from recovering and again becoming threats within a few years was far from clear. The general who had come closest by far was Napoléon (the original, not his nephew) and Moltke knew very well how that had turned out.

Yet the whole tradition of the Prussian/German Army was to accept risks, great risks if need be, to achieve great ends. We can say that Moltke could and should have asked whether this could be taken as a sound or even sane doctrine in these particular circumstances, but what we know of his character gives no reason to imagine that he might have.

At some points during late July 1914 Moltke called insistently for war and seemed confident of winning it. We cannot truly convict him of starting the war for as we've seen it would have been virtually impossible for Germany to stay out once Russia mobilized. Indeed France mobilized before she knew that Germany would mobilize. Germany could not stand by while two hostile states allied against her were mobilizing on her borders.

What Moltke does have a great deal to answer for is how Germany proceeded once mobilization had begun. In particular he bears heavy responsibility not only for the invasion of Belgium but to the terror campaign waged by German forces to facilitate their passage. Even if we were to restrict ourselves to judging him in purely Bismarckian *Realpolitik* terms this was an error of the gravest magnitude that was very costly to Germany in the longer term—to say nothing of the damage it did to the whole fabric of European civilization.

(Of course the responsibility for the terror campaign rests more immediately with the commanders of the armies whose troops waged it. Following World War II some Axis generals were convicted and punished for failing to stop comparable systematic atrocities and it would surely have been better if some World War I German commanders had suffered for the Belgian atrocities, *pour encourager les autres.*)

. . .

VIRTUALLY ALL OF THE German field army commanders and chiefs of staff contributed to diminishing whatever chance there was of winning a resounding victory in the West by failing to heed the lessons of two decades and more of staff rides and war games under both Schlieffen and Moltke. These had taught that to win battles without substantial numerical superiority it was essential to avoid frontal assaults except as part of a scheme of maneuver to envelop one or both of the enemy's flanks deeply enough to prevent him simply from pulling back. Instead they were prone simply to attack at every opportunity that presented.

This was the golden age of the General Staff's power and prestige. Every commander of a higher formation had a General Staff officer as his chief of staff, and he was required to hear him out. Not necessarily to follow the staff chief's advice but to listen—with the obvious implication that if things went wrong the commander might be called to account for failing to heed good counsel. What's more, most higher commanders were themselves General Staff officers and the others usually received especially strong officers as chief of staff.

Yet officers who had performed very well in exercises failed to meet anything like the same operational standard in August-September 1914. Much the same can be said of Moltke himself. Clearly, all their preparation (and in many cases prior combat experience) notwithstanding, these officers were unable to penetrate the Clausewitzian fog of war far enough to permit them to develop and execute the deep operational envelopments of enemy formations that the Schlieffen-Moltke doctrine demanded. Lacking forces with a mobility advantage and the reconnaissance and communications to guide them, they would have had to foresee enemy movements days in advance to do what Schlieffen had demanded of them and they couldn't meet that standard.

· · ·

IN ADDRESSING THEIR OFFICERS the leaders of the General Staff made it clear that they recognized the risk involved in all military plans. They spoke in broad terms of the balance between risk and payoff, and of the need to accept risk in order to achieve their objectives.

What they seem never to have done was to analyze just how much risk their plans might entail or to explicitly weigh alternative plans offering different balances of risk and payoff.

The Great General Staff can be likened to a surgeon who only operated when there was a threat to the life of his patient, the Imperial state. It was tempting to think of the results in simple binary terms: survive or perish. But the patient's health was imperfect to begin with as he suffered from a variety of infirmities and non-military threats to health. While it was possible that he could survive either in reduced or enhanced health he also might die under the GGS's ministrations (as ultimately the Imperial state did in 1918).

The patient might be informed of the potential outcomes and their probabilities under various options so that he could make an informed choice. In practice surgeons often feel sure that they're best able to make the right choice and simply announce it. Frequently the patient is left with misleading impressions regarding the implications, and often surgeons themselves overestimate their own powers and are quick to choose the first option their experience suggests without carefully weighing the risks and payoffs of possible alternatives. This was very much the situation of the GGS surgeon and the monarchical patient on the eve of war.

· · ·

BY ALMOST ANY STANDARD, the Prussian Great General Staff was one of the best planning organizations that ever existed. Its officers were rigorously selected, superbly trained and highly motivated. The GGS studied the same fundamental problem of two-front defense for more than 40 years, free of external constraint or interference.

And it failed. Not only did its plan not achieve the objective but it was not as good as it could have been.

The Great General Staff had greatly and generally violated the Bismarck Law of Chess. In 1857, long before his rise to supreme power, Bismarck wrote to an important political patron and mentor,

> Sympathies and antipathies with regard to foreign powers and persons I cannot reconcile with my concept of duty in the ... service of my country, neither in myself nor in others. There is in them the germ of disloyalty to the lord or the land which one serves .... As long as each of us believes that a part of the chess board is closed to us by our own choice or that we have an arm tied where others can use both arms to our disadvantage, they will make use of our kindness without fear and without thanks.[5]

There can be little doubt that Bismarck would have insisted on the same strictures regarding any options of any kind however outré or contrary to "principle": all must be considered dispassionately.

Such statements are sometimes cited as evidence that Bismarck was utterly unprincipled and cynical but that's not at all accurate. He had strong, passionately-held views, and standards and principles, but he applied them after analyzing the options and issues thoroughly, not in excluding certain tools and moves from use at the outset.

But this could compel him to face the question of the balance between a principle and the benefits to be gained from a policy not strictly constrained by it. It could lead him if not to abandon a principle altogether, then to reshape or shave it for the greater overall benefit as he saw it. That is to say that he never was absolutely unprincipled, as some enemies and former friends furiously charged, but his principles were never absolute.

The General Staff had absolute principles, real even if not explicit and acknowledged. Its highest duty, its officers told themselves, was to the monarchy. Yet in adhering to its absolute principles the GGS cast plans that resulted in the destruction of the monarchy. Thus loyalty to principle involved a great measure of disloyalty to the lord and land which the GGS served much as Bismarck had warned.

Without even thinking about it or deliberately weighing the issues it would appear the GGS closed to consideration large areas of the planning chessboard. Doctrinal and force changes to take full advantage of technological solutions to the well-recognized problems of mobility, reconnaissance and communications; strategic and operational approaches that did not at first sight promise "decisive" results; measures that were not of a strictly "military" character—all these vast swaths of the board were *terrarum interdictis*, squares where the GGS could not or would not consider venturing.

Even setting aside the question of loyalty to the Hohenzollern monarchy, to many in our time—most, probably—it would seem that the blind guides of the GGS had strained at gnats of principle and swallowed camels of aggression and terror against Belgium.

. . .

MUCH HAS CHANGED since 1914. European states are no longer perpetually fearful of attack and no longer keep powerful forces constantly at the ready. European general staffs have ceased to plan continually to mount and repel invasions. For the first time since the fall of Rome there seem to be good prospects of enduring peace in what was the most war-racked region of the world for more than 15 centuries.

At the same time the increasing scale of government and private institutions of all kinds has made the work of general-staff-like planning organizations ever more prominent and critical. Few people who are in a good position to judge would contend that modern top-level planning bodies whether in government or elsewhere are substantially superior to the Prussian Great General Staff. Most are smaller and more constrained in their operation. Their staffs are not more thoroughly trained and prepared nor more strongly motivated. Information technology permits the use of large databases but in many cases it's questionable how much that improves the underlying quality of the planning.

For all that has changed it remains true that we plan with minds decisively shaped by the thousands of millennia that our ancestors lived in groups rarely comprising even as many as half a hundred individuals striving to band together and find the narrow path to survival and prosperity, in a world whose manifold dangers and opportunities could only be dimly perceived. A world where they could live an average of no more than a quarter-century, stalked always by death and terrible loss. A world that sometimes yielded only to extreme caution and at others to unlimited boldness. A world whose limitations drove them to compete desperately yet demanded that they cooperate without reservation.[6]

We are those same creatures still. Nevertheless we live in a very different world built by our immediate ancestors over the past ten millennia, a world in which we feel reasonably sure and comfortable despite its divergences from all that dominated human evolutionary history. The change came in an instant of evolutionary time and we adapt to it by modifying our minds, the minds shaped by evolution in a different environment, modifying them through learned behaviors developed and transmitted over no more than a few hundred generations, with only a little biological evolution.

With these culturally-modified minds we have built a world safer and more comfortable than any our ancestors knew. Or so it seems. Yet we still keen for the simplicities and certainties of the world we have left behind, somewhere in the past, just beyond reach. We could not bear to desert the comforts of our new world yet fear its complexities, seek somehow to turn them back.

And all the while our increasing mastery of the threats that so tormented and bled our forebears has tilted the balance from caution toward boldness. We erect greater and more powerful mechanisms, aspiring to greater mastery, even as we fear that the complexities of what we have already created are overmastering us.[7]

Knowledge is not the key, not in itself. Knowledge is very important, we need more of it but it was not lack of knowledge that prevented the officers of the Great General Staff from better addressing Germany's security problems. They knew almost all of what they needed to and could reasonably have suspected the rest; their failure was in application.

More of us than not it seems fear and recoil from the institutions of gigantism that shadow our world: big government, big banking, big industry, big cities, big technology, big armies. Even those who govern one of them and feel as if they have it under their control generally are apprehensive about most of the others. All the same the scale of human institutions continues to grow inexorably and irreversibly. Efforts to scale back or split up big governments, big

banks, big industries, and the rest, are repeatedly launched with determination and enthusiasm, but almost invariably fail.

Bigness is often explained in terms of economies of scale. Yet as
the studies in this series show big institutions are more prone to
failure than smaller ones largely because of the problems of directing their affairs prudently. In war it is clear that even a moderately
good big army will usually overcome a small one of high quality and
broadly comparable power relationships explain much of gigantism
in many areas. The tendency toward ever-larger institutions of all
kinds has been proceeding with few interruptions over roughly 300
human generations and has accelerated recently.[8] The potentials for
changing this impressively sustained trend will be explored at some
length in the summary volume of this series but the overall prospects are not bright.

If our institutions continue to grow we must change our minds.
Our natural minds cannot deal with the complexities of guiding
what our culturally-modified and expanded minds have made. We
must expand our minds more to master what we have created and
are creating, expand them to help guide us in the process of creation.
That's what this series of studies is all about.[9]

Notes

I. Introduction

[1]   Keegan, John, *The First World War* (New York: Knopf, 1998), p. 28.

[2]   Some ripe examples of Schlieffen idolatry are quoted in Mombauer, Annika, *Helmuth von Moltke and the Origins of the First World War* (Cambridge: Cambridge University Press, 2001), pp. 3-4.

[3]   Major historians who appear to continue to stand guard on this camp include Max Hastings and Holger Herwig, while the most commanding proponent remains the late Fritz Fischer.

[4]   Lambelet, André José, "Manifestly Inferior? French Reserves, 1871-1914," in *Scraping the Barrel: The Military Use of Sub-Standard Manpower*, ed. Sanders Marble (New York: Fordham University Press, 2012).

II. Prussia and Empire

[1]   For the history of Prussia, see Clark, Christopher, *Iron Kingdom: The Rise and Downfall of Prussia, 1600–1947* (London: Penguin Books, 2007).

[2]   Clark, *Iron Kingdom*, p. 215.

[3]   Steinberg, Jonathan, *Bismarck: A Life* (Oxford: Oxford University Press, 2011) is my main source for Bismarck.

[4]   Emil Volkers, *Wilhelm I auf dem Weg zur Frontinspektion*, 1872.

[5]   For an overview of Bismarck's policies see Snyder, Jack [L], *Myths of Empire: Domestic Politics and International Ambition* (Ithaca: Cornell University Press, 1991), pp. 68-69 & 82-84.

6   Based on *"The German (North German) Confederation, 1815 to 1870,"* copyright *IEG-Maps - Kartenserver am Institut für Europäische Geschichte Mainz*, used with permission.

III. Prussia's Military System

1   Good books on Prussia's military system are too numerous to mention, but Citino, Robert M., *The German Way of War: From the Thirty Years' War to the Third Reich* (Lawrence, Kansas: University of Kansas Press, 2005) provides an overview with many references. Also valuable for the period after 1870 has been Brose, Eric Dorn, *The Kaiser's Army: The Politics of Military Technology in Germany During the Machine Age, 1870–1914* (Oxford: Oxford University Press, 2001). For a good succinct account see Stevenson, David, *Armaments and the Coming of War: Europe, 1904–1915* (Oxford: Clarendon Press, 1996), pp. 40-47. For an informed and thoughtful briefer survey see Showalter, Dennis, "From Deterrence to Doomsday Machine: The German Way of War, 1890–1914," *The Journal of Military History* 64, No. 3 (Jul 2000): 679-710.

2   There are many accounts of the General Staff of varying quality and focus. Among the better are Bucholz, Arden, *Moltke, Schlieffen, and Prussian War Planning* (New York: Berg, 1991) and Mombauer, *Helmuth von Moltke and the Origins of the First World War*, pp. 14-41. Christian O. E. Millotat, a senior officer of the modern German General Staff (later a *Generalmajor*), has written a valuable survey, *Understanding the Prussian-German General Staff System* (Carlisle Barracks, Pennsylvania: Strategic Studies Institute, U.S. Army War College, 20 Mar 1992). Also see Echevarria, Antulio J., II, *After Clausewitz: German Military Thinkers Before the Great War* (Lawrence, Kansas: University of Kansas Press, 2000) and Citino, *The German Way of War*, both with much about the GGS. Bronsart von Schellendorff, Paul and Friedrich, *The Duties of the General Staff*, trans. H. A. Bethell, J. H. V. Crowe, and F. B. Maurice, Fourth ed. (London: His Majesty's Stationary Office, 1905) explains the specific duties of the General Staff officer.

3   For the contrast in the experience of battle between 1815 and 1916 see Keegan, John, *The Face of Battle: A Study of Agincourt, Waterloo, and the Somme* (New York: Viking Press, 1976), chapters 3 and 4.

4   That this was the essence of Prussia's top-level military strategy and had been since the 1700s is the central thesis of Citino, *The German Way of War*.

5   Bucholz, Arden, *Moltke and the German Wars, 1864–1871* (London: Palgrave, 2001) outlines Moltke's career. Also illuminating is Hughes, Daniel J., ed., *Moltke on the Art of War: Selected Writings* (New York: Presidio Press, 1993).

6   Hughes, ed., *Moltke on the Art of War*, p. 3.

[7]   Bucholz, *Moltke, Schlieffen, and Prussian War Planning*, pp. 40-41.
[8]   For Moltke's thinking see Hughes, ed., *Moltke on the Art of War*, especially pp. 171-224.
[9]   Cron, Hermann, *Imperial German Army, 1914–18: Organisation, Structure, Orders of Battle*, trans. C.F. Colton (Solihull, West Midlands: Helion, 1937, 2002), Chapter B.4., Amazon Kindle location 1874.
[10]   Bucholz, *Moltke, Schlieffen, and Prussian War Planning*, p. 302. Kuhl, General [Hermann J.] von and General [Walter F. A.] von Bergmann, *Movements and Supply of the German First Army During August and September, 1914* (Fort Leavenworth: Command and General Staff School Press, 1929), pp. 2-4. Bronsart, *The Duties of the General Staff*, pp. 236, 353-54. Zuber, Terence, *The Battle of the Frontiers: Ardennes, 1914* (Stroud, Gloucestershire: The History Press, 2013), Amazon Kindle location 616.
[11]   For more on German military superiority see Dupuy, Trevor N., *A Genius for War: The German Army and General Staff, 1807–1945* (Garden City, New York: Military Book Club, 2002; Prentice-Hall, 1977), pp. 177-78, 290-99, 328-32. Some caution is in order as the apparent precision in DuPuy's measures of effectiveness is spurious due to mathematical inconsistencies and the incorporation of subjective judgment but there is value in what he says even allowing for this. Also worthwhile is Zuber, *The Battle of the Frontiers: Ardennes, 1914*, which compares German and French tactical preparation in some depth.
[12]   Zuber, *The Battle of the Frontiers: Ardennes, 1914*, Amazon Kindle locations 287-292.
[13]   The trajectory of Moltke's thinking has been most clearly analyzed by Stig Förster in two articles: "Facing 'People's War': Moltke the Elder and Germany's Military Options After 1871," *Journal of Strategic Studies* 10, No. 2 (1987): 209-30, and "Dreams and Nightmares: German Military Leadership and the Images of Future Warfare, 1871–1914," in *Anticipating Total War: The German and American Experiences, 1871–1914*, ed. Manfred F. Boemeke and Roger Chickering (Cambridge: Cambridge University Press, 1999).
[14]   Ritter, Gerhard, *The Schlieffen Plan: Critique of a Myth* (London: Oswald Wolff, 1958), p. 18.
[15]   Förster, "Dreams and Nightmares", p. 347.

iv. In the Reign of the Last Kaiser

[1]   My picture of Wilhelm's character and its political effects rests fundamentally on Kohut, Thomas A., *Wilhelm II and the Germans: A Study in Leadership* (Oxford: Oxford University Press, 1991) as well as Röhl, John C. G., *The Kaiser and His Court: Wilhelm II and the Government of Germany*, trans. Terence F. Cole (Cambridge: Cambridge University Press, 1994). Re-

garding Wilhelm and the business of the Army he commanded see Stevenson, *Armaments and the Coming of War*, p. 42.

[2]   By Max Koner, 1891.

[3]   Geyer, Dietrich, *Russian Imperialism: The Integration of Domestic and Foreign Policy, 1860–1914*, trans. Bruce Little (New Haven: Yale University Press, 1987), pp. 150-58.

[4]   For an extended treatment of the frictions and their effects on British views see Kennedy, Paul M., *The Rise of the Anglo-German Antagonism, 1860–1914* (Amherst: Humanity Books, 1980. A succinct summary is provided in Harris, J. Paul, "Great Britain," in *The Origins of World War I*, ed. Richard F. Hamilton and Holger H. Herwig (Cambridge: Cambridge University Press, 2003), Amazon Kindle locations 6744 et seq.

[5]   Data from Broadberry, Stephen and Alexander Klein, "Aggregate and Per Capita GDP in Europe, 1870-2000: Continental, Regional and National Data With Changing Boundaries," *Scandinavian Economic History Review* 60, No. 1 (Mar 2012): 79–107, supplementary data.

[6]   From Ferguson, Niall, *The Pity of War* (New York: Basic Books, 1998), p. 92 [which is based on German estimates], except British mobilized strength from *Statistics of the Military Effort of the British Empire During the Great War, 1914–1920* (London: War Office, Mar 1922), p. 228.

[7]   Bushnell, John, "The Tsarist Officer Corps, 1881–1914: Customs, Duties, Inefficiency," *The American Historical Review* 86, No. 4 (Oct 1981): 753-80. Stevenson, *Armaments*, pp. 51-54, 76-80, 151.

[8]   Based on data from Broadberry and Klein, "Aggregate and Per Capita GDP in Europe."

[9]   From Herrmann, David G., *The Arming of Europe and the Making of the First World War* (Princeton: Princeton University Press, 1996), p. 237, except Serbia figure from Palairet, Michael, "Fiscal Pressure and Peasant Impoverishment in Serbia before World War I," *Journal of Economic History* 39, No. 3 (Sep 1979): 719-40, p. 721. Converted to dollars and inflated to 1990 prices using GDP deflator from Officer, Lawrence H. and Samuel H. Williamson, "Computing 'Real Value' Over Time With a Conversion Between U.K. Pounds and U.S. Dollars, 1830 to Present," *MeasuringWorth*, 2013.

[10]   Stone, Norman. *The Eastern Front, 1914–1917* (London: Penguin, 1975, 2005), pp. 17-58.

[11]   Fuller, William C., Jr., *Strategy and Power in Russia, 1600–1914* (New York: Free Press, 1992), pp. 450-51.

[12]   Wohlforth, William C., "The Perception of Power: Russia in the Pre–1914 Balance," *World Politics* 39, No. 3 (Apr 1987): 353-81.

[13]   Herwig, Holger H., "Imperial Germany," in *Knowing One's Enemies: Intelligence Assessment Before the Two World Wars*, ed. Ernest R. May (Princeton: Princeton University Press, 1984): 62-97.

[14] Deák, István, *Beyond Nationalism: A Social and Political History of the Habsburg Officer Corps, 1848–1918* (New York: Oxford University Press, 1990). Stevenson, *Armaments*, pp. 47-51, 80-86.

[15] Stevenson, *Armaments*, pp. 89-90. Herrmann, *Arming of Europe*, pp. 299-301.

[16] Zuber, *The Battle of the Frontiers: Ardennes, 1914*, Amazon Kindle locations 486 et seq.

[17] For World War I artillery generally see Hogg, Ian V., *The Guns, 1914–18* (New York: Ballantine Books, 1971), as well as Jäger, Herbert, *German Artillery of World War One* (Marlborough, Wiltshire: Crowood Press, 2001) specifically for German artillery. Zuber, *The Battle of the Frontiers: Ardennes, 1914* offers a good description of the operational employment and characteristics of artillery at Amazon Kindle locations 937–1130.

[18] Zuber, Terence, *The Real German War Plan, 1904–1914* (Stroud, Gloucestershire: The History Press, 2011), Amazon Kindle location 1736.

[19] For early development of military aviation see Morrow, John H., Jr., *The Great War in the Air: Military Aviation from 1909 to 1921* (Washington: Smithsonian Institution Press, 1993). Morrow sketches events prior to 1909 as well as covering those of World War I.

[20] An observation I owe to the late Charles William Wahl, M.D., a prominent psychoanalyst and student of the classics.

[21] Dale, Henry, *Early Flying Machines* (London: The British Library, 1992).

[22] Laux, James M., *The European Automobile Industry* (New York: Twayne Publishers, 1992), pp. 2-22.

[23] Brooks, Peter W., *Historic Airships* (Greenwich, Connecticut: New York Graphic Society, 1973), *passim*, and Robinson, Douglas H., *Giants in the Sky: A History of the Rigid Airship* (Seattle: University of Washington Press, 1973), pp. 28-29.

[24] Brose, *Kaiser's Army*, pp. 75-79. Moltke to War Ministry, "Production of airships," 2 Mar 1911, reproduced in Ludendorff, [Erich F.W.], ed., *The General Staff and its Problems*, trans. F.A. Holt, 2 vols. (New York: E. P. Dutton & Co., 1920), pp. 1:32-33.

[25] Themistokles von Eckenbrecher, *Zeppelin über Antwerpen*, 1914.

[26] Idem, *Beschießung einer deutschen Taube*, 1914.

[27] Morrow, John H., Jr., *Building German Airpower, 1909–1914* (Knoxville: University of Tennessee Press, 1976), pp. 1-87.

[28] Brose, *Kaiser's Army*, pp. 138-45.

[29] Humphries, Mark Osborne and John Maker, eds., *Germany's Western Front: Translations from the German Official History of the Great War, 1914: Part 1, The Battle of the Frontiers and the Pursuit to the Marne* (Waterloo, Ontario: Wilfrid Laurier University Press, 2013), Amazon Kindle edition,

Chapter 1, Introduction, section on "The War's Duration and Economic Management."

v. Losing the Peace

[30]   C.R.W. Nevinson, *Column on the March*, 1915.

[1]   Angell, Norman, *The Great Illusion: A Study of the Relation of Military Power to National Advantage*, "New edition" (London: William Heinemann, 1912).

[2]   For the ancient and enduring economic, political, and social backwardness of the Balkans see Chirot, Daniel, ed., *The Origins of Backwardness in Eastern Europe: Economics and Politics from the Middle Ages Until the Early Twentieth Century* (Berkeley: University of California Press, 1989); especially pp. 133-35.

[3]   The mechanisms and processes of Ottoman expansion and stagnation in Europe are most clearly explained by McNeill, William H., *Europe's Steppe Frontier, 1500–1800* (Chicago: University of Chicago Press, 1964). The events are conveniently traced by Hupchick, Dennis P. and Harold E. Cox, *The Palgrave Concise Historical Atlas of the Balkans* (New York: Palgrave, 2001), so far as the Balkans are concerned, and by McEvedy, Colin, *The New Penguin Atlas of Medieval History* and *The Penguin Atlas of Modern History (to 1815)* (London: Penguin Books, 1992 and 1972) for Europe generally.

[4]   Quataert, Donald, *The Ottoman Empire, 1700–1922*, 2nd ed. (Cambridge: Cambridge University Press, 2005) succinctly overviews the long decline. The relationship between the Balkans and the broader currents of European history in the Nineteenth Century is addressed briefly in Blanning, T. C. W., ed., *The Nineteenth Century: Europe 1789–1914*, The Short Oxford History of Europe (Oxford: Oxford University Press, 2000).

[5]   Geyer, *Russian Imperialism*.

[6]   From this point forward in this chapter my basic picture of the events leading up to war is built on Clark, Christopher, *The Sleepwalkers: How Europe Went to War in 1914* (New York: Harper, 2013), together with Hamilton, Richard F. and Holger H. Herwig, eds., *The Origins of World War I* (Cambridge: Cambridge University Press, 2003). My conclusions differ from theirs in some respects, however (and theirs from one another).

[7]   Based on "*South Eastern Europe,*" 1878 and 1914, copyright *IEG-Maps*, used with permission.

[8]   Hall, Richard C., "Serbia," in *Origins of World War I*, ed. Hamilton and Herwig, Amazon Kindle locations 2344 et seq.

[9]   Rich, David Alan, "Russia," in *Origins of World War I*, ed. Hamilton and Herwig, Amazon Kindle locations 4904 et seq.

[10]   Fuller, *Strategy and Power in Russia, 1600–1914*, pp. 418-20.

[11]   Deák, *Beyond Nationalism*. The book ranges well beyond its titular subject for reasons the author explains.

[12]   Regarding Serbia see Clark, *Sleepwalkers*, pp. 3-64. On her economy see Palairet, Michael, *The Balkan Economies, c. 1800–1914: Evolution Without Development* (Cambridge: Cambridge University Press, 1997).

[13]   Tunstall, Graydon A., Jr., "Austria-Hungary," in *Origins of World War I*, ed. Hamilton and Herwig, Amazon Kindle locations 3211 and 3248.

[14]   Hall, Richard C., "Serbia," in *Origins of World War I*, ed. Hamilton and Herwig, Amazon Kindle locations 2552 et seq.

[15]   Clark, *Sleepwalkers*, pp. 29-30.

[16]   Robbins, Keith, "Grey, Edward, Viscount Grey of Fallodon (1862 – 1933)", *Oxford Dictionary of National Biography*, Oxford University Press, 2004; online edn, Jan 2011.

[17]   Robbins, Keith, "Grey, Edward," paraphrasing the reactions to Grey expressed by Beatrice Webb, famous as a social scientist, thinker and reformer.

[18]   Geiss, *July 1914*, documents 73, 80, 82, 85, 93, 128.

[19]   Harris, J. Paul, "Great Britain," in *Origins of World War I*, ed. Hamilton and Herwig, Amazon Kindle locations 6916 et seq., provides considerable detail.

[20]   Grey summarized his arguments in his speech to the House of Commons on August 3, printed in Hansard, *HC Deb 03 August 1914 vol 65* cc1809-32.

[21]   Harris, J. Paul, "Great Britain," in *Origins of World War I*, ed. Hamilton and Herwig, Amazon Kindle locations 6990 et seq.

[22]   For some dissenting voices see Hansard, *HC Deb 03 August 1914 vol 65* cc1833-48.

[23]   Most notably the German historian Fritz Fischer (1908–1999), whose 1961 book *Griff nach der Weltmacht* (*Bid for World Power*, issued in translation as *Germany's Aims in the First World War*) set off an intense and long-running debate in Germany and elsewhere.

[24]   Ferguson, *Pity of War*, pp. 169-72. Regarding Ferguson's conclusions about the benign consequences of a German victory however, see Harris, J. Paul, "Great Britain," in *Origins of World War I*, ed. Hamilton and Herwig, Amazon Kindle locations 7279 et seq.

[25]   Snyder, *Myths of Empire*, p. 86.

[26]   Geiss, *July 1914*, documents 112, 115, 133, and 134; also 143–145.

vi. The Cruelest Month

[1]   Principal sources for this chapter are Humphries & Maker, eds., *Germany's Western Front*; Senior, Ian, *Home Before the Leaves Fall* (Botley, Oxford: Osprey Publishing, 2012); and Zuber, *The Real German War Plan*. Zuber is especially penetrating about the overall shape of the campaigns but he omits or distort critical details, such as the order in which the initial major offensives took place, and his point of view is narrowly German. Sen-

ior's understanding of the nature of the operations is less strong but he does a good job on the details. The Humphries and Osborne book is comprised of selected and annotated translations from the German official operational history, *Der Weltkrieg*, and is the most authoritative source of most details of German operations. Brose, *Kaiser's Army*, is also illuminating on many aspects.

[2]   Zuber, *The Battle of the Frontiers: Ardennes, 1914*, Amazon Kindle location 1893.

[3]   For the natural defenses of France see Johnson, Douglas Wilson, *Topography and Strategy in the War* (New York: Henry Holt & Co., 1917), pp. 1-25.

[4]   The issues of the French Army in the years before the war are dealt with in summary in Porch, Douglas, "The French Army in the First World War," in *Military Effectiveness: Volume I: The First World War*, ed. Allan R. Millett and Williamson Murray (London: Unwin Hyman, 1988), and at greater length in Porch's, *The March to the Marne: The French Army 1871–1914* (Cambridge: Cambridge University Press, 1981; reprint, 2003) as well as Ralston, David B. , *The Army of the Republic: The Place of the Military in the Political Evolution of France, 1871–1914* (Cambridge: MIT Press, 1967). For a good brief summary see Stevenson, *Armaments*, pp. 54-58, 90-96.

[5]   On Joffre and his plans see the first two chapters of Doughty, Robert A., *Pyrrhic Victory: French Strategy and Operations in the Great War* (Cambridge: Belknap Press of Harvard University Press, 2005), as well as his "French Strategy in 1914: Joffre's Own," *Journal of Military History* 67, no. 2 (Apr 2003): 427-54.

[6]   http://www.fortified-places.com/liege/.

[7]   Adapted from Figure 1. of Johnson, *Topography and Strategy*.

[8]   Donnell, Clayton, *The Forts of the Meuse in World War I* (Botley, Oxford: Osprey, 2007) provides the fullest account of the Liège fortifications and their defense.

[9]   Humphries & Maker, eds., *Germany's Western Front* (Kindle Locations 1715-1720). Moltke comments on Schlieffen Plan, 1911(?), trans. in Ritter, *The Schlieffen Plan*, pp. 165-66, and in Zuber, Terence, *German War Planning, 1891–1914: Sources and Interpretations* (Woodbridge, Suffolk: Boydell Press, 2004), pp. 203-04.

[10]   In addition to the accounts in Donnell, *Forts*, see Hogg, *The Guns, 1914–18*, pp. 33-47 regarding the assaults. For the German account see Humphries & Maker, eds., *Germany's Western Front* (Kindle Location 1908 et seq.)

[11]   Regarding the development of German siege artillery and the GGS role see Brose, *Kaiser's Army*, pp. 50-51, 65, 158, & 201-02. For more on the guns see Romanych, Marc and Martin Rupp, *42cm "Big Bertha" and German*

Siege Artillery of World War I (Oxford: Osprey, 2014) as well as Jäger, *German Artillery*, pp. 34-68.

[12] For the perspective of an artilleryman on the employment of the large siege guns see Captain Becker, "The 42-cm. Mortar: Fact and Fancy," [U.S.] *Field Artillery Journal* 12, No. 3 (May-Jun 1922): 224-231, trans. by O. L. Spaulding, Jr. from *Artilleristische Monatshefte*, Jul-Aug 1921.

[13] Herwig, Holger H., *The Marne, 1914: The Opening of World War I and the Battle That Changed the World* (New York: Random House, 2009), pp. 123-24.

[14] For differing assessments of how much the Belgians delayed the advance see Donnell, *Forts*, pp. 53-54.

[15] Senior, *Home Before the Leaves Fall*, Amazon Kindle locations 1130-43.

[16] Zuber, *The Battle of the Frontiers: Ardennes, 1914*. Herwig, *The Marne, 1914*, pp. 145-51. Humphries & Maker, eds., *Germany's Western Front* (Kindle Locations 4406–18).

[17] Beckett, Ian F. W., "French, John Denton Pinkstone, first earl of Ypres (1852 –1925)," *Oxford Dictionary of National Biography*, Oxford University Press, 2004; online edn.

[18] Edmonds, James E., *Military Operations: France and Belgium, 1914, History of the Great War, Based on Official Documents* (London: Macmillan, 1937), pp. 50-52.

[19] Humphries & Maker, eds., *Germany's Western Front* (Kindle Locations 5360-62).

[20] Humphries & Maker, eds., *Germany's Western Front* (Kindle Locations 2839-45, 2928-49).

[21] The system of shared command it explained best by Millotat, *Understanding the Prussian-German General Staff System*.

[22] Schniewindt, [Rudolph], "Signal Communication Between the Headquarters Staffs During the Warfare of Movement in 1914," *The Signal Corps Bulletin*, No. 74 (Sep-Oct 1933): 1-26, p. 8.

[23] Humphries & Maker, eds., *Germany's Western Front* (Kindle Locations 3044-85).

VII. Schlieffen's Daring Idea

[1] Together, Mombauer, Annika, "Of War Plans and War Guilt: The Debate Surrounding the Schlieffen Plan," *Journal of Strategic Studies* 28, No. 5 (Oct 2005): 857-85; Foley, Robert T., "The Real Schlieffen Plan," *War in History* 13, No. 1 (2006): 91–115; and Groß, Gerhard P., "There Was a Schlieffen Plan: New Sources on the History of German Military Planning," *War in History* 15, No. 4 (2008): 389-431 can serve as a prosecutorial summary of the charges of historiographical malfeasance and misfeasance against Zuber. For his rebuttal see, "The 'Schlieffen Plan' and German War Guilt," *War in History* 14, No. 1 (2007): 96–108; Zuber, "Everybody Knows There

Was a 'Schlieffen Plan': A Reply to Annika Mombauer," *War in History* 15, No. 1 (Jan 2008): 92–101; and Zuber, "There Never Was a 'Schlieffen Plan': A Reply to Gerhard Gross," *War in History* 17, No. 2 (Apr 2010): 231-49.

2   Zuber's most attractive and accessible presentation of his basic ideas is his "The Schlieffen Plan: Fantasy or Catastrophe?" *History Today* 52, No. 9 (Sep 2002): 40-46. The place to start in understanding his research results is *The Real German War Plan*. This in part duplicates *Inventing the Schlieffen Plan: German War Planning 1871–1914* (Oxford: Oxford University Press, 2003), but the earlier work also contains other material that serious students will want to see. Zuber engaged in a running (and frequently acrimonious) debate on some points with several historians over the period from 1999 to 2011, mostly in the pages of *War in History*. He provides a résumé from his perspective, with references to all of the original articles, at www.terencezuber.com/schlieffendebate.html.

3   Regarding Schlieffen's background and career see Bucholz, *Moltke, Schlieffen, and Prussian War Planning*, pp. 109–134 & *passim*, as well as *Neue deutsche Biografie*, Vol, 23 (Berlin, 2003), pp. 81-83. Ritter, *The Schlieffen Plan*, pp. 98f, paints a vivid portrait. For selected writings see Foley, Robert T., ed. & trans., *Alfred von Schlieffen's Military Writings* (London: Frank Cass, 2003).

4   For inconsistent figures see Bucholz, *Moltke, Schlieffen, and Prussian War Planning*, pp. 137, 224; Millotat, *Understanding the Prussian-German General Staff System*, pp. 39-40 ; Mombauer, *Helmuth von Moltke*, p. 25; and Samuels, Martin, *Command or Control? Command, Training and Tactics in the British and German Armies, 1888–1918* (London: Frank Cass, 1995), p. 15. On p. 37 Mombauer says that "only about ten candidates per annual intake would finally end up as General Staff officers," which would imply that the total could not exceed 300 active-duty officers at most. For the needs for field formations see Bronsart, *The Duties of the General Staff*, pp. 255 et seq.

5   Mombauer, *Helmuth von Moltke*, pp. 42-46.

6   Regarding the younger Moltke's background and career see Mombauer, *Helmuth von Moltke*, pp. 47-72; Bucholz, *Moltke, Schlieffen, and Prussian War Planning*, pp. 109–134; and *Neue deutsche Biografie*, Vol, 18 (Berlin, 1997), pp. 17–18.

7   The text is available in translation in Foley, *Schlieffen's Military Writings*, pp. 163-79; Ritter, *Schlieffen Plan*, pp. 134-66 or Zuber, *German War Planning, 1891–1914*, pp. 187-204. All include a 1906 addendum, while Ritter and Zuber add Moltke's comments, apparently from 1911. Ritter also offers copies of the drafts and of a selection of the sketch maps which accompanied the memo, although their precise relation to it is not clear.

8   Zuber, *The Real German War Plan*, Amazon Kindle locations 1114 et seq.

[9] Notably Robert T. Foley in his "The Real Schlieffen Plan."

[10] See Zuber's critique, "The 'Schlieffen Plan' and German War Guilt."

[11] Zuber, Terence, "The Schlieffen Plan's 'Ghost Divisions' March Again: A Reply to Terence Holmes," *War in History* 17, No. 4 (Nov 2010): 512-25, pp. 513, 515 (n. 8). Zuber, "Everybody Knows There Was a 'Schlieffen Plan,'" p. 99. Zuber, "The 'Schlieffen Plan' and German War Guilt," p. 107.

[12] Zuber, Terence, "There Never Was a 'Schlieffen Plan': A Reply to Gerhard Gross," *War in History* 17, No. 2 (Apr 2010): 231-49.

[13] Bundesarchiv, Bild 183–1986-0425-500, May 1916.

[14] On Groener, see Stoneman, Mark R., *Wilhelm Groener, Officering, and the Schlieffen Plan* (Ph.D. diss., Georgetown University, 2006) and *Neue deutsche Biografie*, Vol. 7 (Berlin, 1966), pp. 111–114. The outlines of his career in various works by Terrence Zuber are unreliable.

[15] Goodspeed, D. J., *Ludendorff: Genius of World War I* (Boston: Houghton Mifflin, 1966), p. 13.

[16] Zuber, "The 'Schlieffen Plan' and German War Guilt," p. 96.

[17] Mombauer, *Helmuth von Moltke*, p. 100.

[18] Stoneman, *Wilhelm Groener*, pp. 187-91, 195–197.

[19] Stoneman, *Wilhelm Groener*, p. 195.

[20] Mombauer, "Of War Plans and War Guilt," p. 878.

VIII. The Flaws of the Perfect Plan

[1] Zuber helpfully offers a selection of translations from important articles and books by GGS officers, as well as Delbrück, in *German War Planning, 1891–1914*, pp. 296-301.

[2] Cron, *Imperial German Army, 1914–18*, App. I, Amazon Kindle location 6951 et seq.

[3] In 1920 Gerhard Tappen, who had been Moltke's operations chief in 1914, published a book in which he contended that there was no room in Northern Belgium for more troops. Hermann von Kuhl, who had been chief of staff for the German First Army, insisted there had been. Both men were defending their records. In essence I conclude that Tappen had the better argument, albeit on somewhat different grounds. See Zuber, *Inventing the Schlieffen Plan*, n. 37 (p. 26).

[4] Zuber, *The Battle of the Frontiers: Ardennes, 1914*, Amazon Kindle location 586.

IX. Making It Work—Maybe

[1] Noce, Daniel, "Strategic Demolitions of Railroads in Front of the German Right Wing, August-September 1914," (Washington: War Department, Office of the Chief of Engineers, Mar 1940).

[2] On the development of powered vehicles, generally and for military use, see Eckermann, Erik, *World History of the Automobile* (Warrendale, Pennsylvania: Society of Automotive Engineers, 2001); Ellis, Chris, *Military*

Transport of World War I (Poole, Dorset, England: Blandford Press, 1970) and Laux, *European Automobile Industry.*

[3]   The trade press of the period published many data on truck costs, showing little divergence; this represents typical figures. Converted to dollars (where necessary) and inflated to 1990 prices using GDP deflator from Officer and Williamson, "Computing 'Real Value' Over Time."

[4]   Broadberry and Klein, "Aggregate and Per Capita GDP in Europe, 1870-2000," supplementary data.

[5]   Moody, Lucian B., "Motor Transport for Field Artillery," *Field Artillery Journal* 6 (1916): 25-42.

[6]   Laux, *The European Automobile Industry*, p. 44.

[7]   "Fifteen Makers Get War Premium," *The Automobile* [New York], Sep 10, 1915, p. 493.

[8]   Laux, James M., "Trucks in the West During the First World War," *Journal of Transport History* 6, No. 2 (Dec 1985): 64-70, p. 67.

[9]   Humphries & Maker, eds., *Germany's Western Front* (Kindle Locations 7548, 7563-66).

[10]   Herwig, *The Marne, 1914*, p. 262.

[11]   Stevenson, *Armaments*, p. 10, fn. 15.

[12]   Stevenson, *Armaments*, p. 7.

[13]   Mombauer, *Helmuth von Moltke and the Origins of the First World War*, p. 22.

[14]   Humphries & Maker, eds., *Germany's Western Front* (Kindle Locations 2173-75, 2193-95). Zuber, *The Battle of the Frontiers: Ardennes, 1914*, Amazon Kindle locations 2053-69.

[15]   Morrow, John H., Jr., "Industrial Mobilization in World War I: The Prussian Army and the Aircraft Industry," *Journal of Economic History* 37, No. 1 (Mar 1977): 36-51.

[16]   Munson, Kenneth, *Pioneer Aircraft, 1903–1914* (New York: Macmillan, 1969). Wagner, Ray and Heinz Nowarra, *German Combat Planes* (Garden City, New York: Doubleday & Co., 1971), pp. 4–11.

[17]   Wagner and Nowarra, *German Combat Planes*, p. 112.

[18]   Schlosberg, R[ichard] T., "A Study of the Time Required for Complete Dissemination of Orders of Large Units for Tactical Operations, to the Lowest Echelons, Based Upon Historical Examples of the World War," Individual Research Papers, (Fort Leavenworth: Command and General Staff School, 1936), p. 27.

[19]   Humphries & Maker, eds., *Germany's Western Front* (Kindle Locations 2588-96, 2890-2901).

[20]   Afflerbach, Holger, "Wilhelm II as Supreme Warlord in the First World War," *War in History* 5, No. 4 (Oct 1998): 427-49, pp. 433-34.

[21]   Sherman, William T., *Memoirs*, 2 vols. (New York: D. Appleton & Co., 1875), p. 2:398.

[22]   The main sources on German communications in 1914 are Schniewindt, "Signal Communication Between the Headquarters Staffs" and Evans, Paul W., "Strategic Signal Communication—A Study of Signal Communication as Applied to Large Field Forces, Based Upon the Operations of the German Signal Corps During the March on Paris in 1914," *The* [U.S.] *Signal Corps Bulletin*, No. 82 (Jan-Feb 1935): 24-58. Also useful are Schlosberg, "A Study of the Time Required for Complete Dissemination of Orders," and Section IV.I.1 of Cron, *Imperial German Army, 1914–18*. Regarding technical issues I have relied a good deal on my own technical knowledge.

[23]   Humphries & Maker, eds., *Germany's Western Front* (Kindle Locations 4557-63).

[24]   Explained clearly in Millotat, *Understanding the Prussian-German General Staff System.*

[25]   Humphries & Maker, eds., *Germany's Western Front* (Kindle Locations 4564-4623).

[26]   Zuber, *The Battle of the Frontiers: Ardennes, 1914*, Amazon Kindle location 268.

[27]   Zuber, *The Battle of the Frontiers: Ardennes, 1914*, Amazon Kindle locations 1411-40.

[28]   Clausewitz, Carl von, *On War*, trans. Michael Howard and Peter Paret (New York: Everyman's Library, 1984, 1832), p. 319.

x. Delusions of Strategy

[1]   Horne, John and Alan Kramer, *German Atrocities, 1914: A History of Denial* (New Haven, Conn.: Yale University Press, 2002). Lipkes, Jeff, *Rehearsals: The German Army in Belgium, August 1914* (Leuven, Belgium: Leuven University Press, 2007).

[2]   Geiss, *July 1914*, document 91.

[3]   Lipkes, Jeff, "Rehearsals: The German Army in Belgium, August 1914: Afterword," http://www.jefflipkes.com/files/Afterwor1.pdf for motivations.

[4]   Bergin, Joseph, ed., *The Seventeenth Century: Europe 1598–1715*, The Short Oxford History of Europe (Oxford: Oxford University Press, 2001), pp. 9–10, 21, 112-25.

[5]   E.g,, Groß, "There Was a Schlieffen Plan," p. 426, quoting Schlieffen.

[6]   Zuber, *Real German War Plan* (Kindle Locations 3519-20). Except as noted, all the generalizations here about the lessons of prewar exercises and war games rely on this study.

[7]   Snyder, *Myths of Empire*, pp. 7 & 72.

[8]   Published in *Deutsche Revue*, Jan 1909.

[9]   Foley, *Alfred von Schlieffen's Military Writings*, pp. 202-05.

¹⁰   Foley, *Alfred von Schlieffen's Military Writings*, p. 186. For an objective summary of some critical aspects of the actual situation see Snyder, *Myths of Empire*, pp. 70-72 & 76-77.

¹¹   Moltke to Bethmann Hollweg, 21 Dec 1912, reproduced in Ludendorff, ed., *The General Staff and its Problems*, pp. 1:57-69, pp. 61-62.

¹²   Letter dated September 7, quoted in Mombauer, *Helmuth von Moltke and the Origins of the First World War*, p. 288.

¹³   Broadberry, Stephen and Mark Harrison, eds., *The Economics of World War I* (Cambridge: Cambridge University Press, 2005).

¹⁴   Herwig, Holger H., "Germany," in *Origins of World War I*, ed. Hamilton and Herwig, Amazon Kindle locations 4263 et seq.

¹⁵   On Austria-Hungary and her army see Clark, *Sleepwalkers*, pp. 65–117 and Deák, *Beyond Nationalism*. On the Austro-Hungarian Army and its infirmities, and the follies of its leaders see Stone, *Eastern Front*.

¹⁶   Stone, N[orman], "Moltke and Conrad: Relations Between the Austro-Hungarian and German General Staffs, 1909–1914," in *The War Plans of the Great Powers, 1890–1914*, ed. Paul M. Kennedy (Boston: Allen & Unwin, 1979, 1966) pp. 222-251.

XI. What Were They *Thinking*?

¹   O'Neil, William D. *What Were They* Thinking? http://whatweretheythinking.williamdoneil.com/

²   *Deutsche Biografie*, http://www.deutsche-biographie.de/, s.v. "Thomsen, Hermann Christian Johannes," cites both versions of his name. His pre-war GGS work is sketched in Morrow, *Building German Airpower, 1909–1914*, pp. 14–15, 43, and throughout pp. 1-87. There are also numerous references to Thomsen and his work in aviation in this era scattered through pp. 1-57 of Morrow, *The Great War in the Air*. His service record is outlined at http://home.comcast.net/~jcviser/aka/lieth.htm.

³   Roeingh, Rolf, *Flieger des Weltkrieges: „der junge Riese reckt sich"*, Vol. 2 (Berlin: Deutschen Archiv Verlag, 1941), pp. 29-34.

⁴   For military decision-making in Wilhelmine Germany see Mombauer, *Helmuth von Moltke and the Origins of the First World War*, pp. 14-41.

⁵   Quoted in Steinberg, *Bismarck*, p. 131.

⁶   Bowles, Samuel and Herbert Gintis, *A Cooperative Species: Human Reciprocity and Its Evolution* (Princeton: Princeton University Press, 2011).

⁷   Levy, Jonathan Ira, *Freaks of Fortune: The Emerging World of Capitalism and Risk in America* (Cambridge: Harvard University Press, 2012).

⁸   Nolan, Patrick and Gerhard Lenski, *Human Societies: An Introduction to Macrosociology*, Ninth ed. (Boulder: Paradigm, 2004).

⁹   O'Neil, *What Were They* Thinking?

Bibliography

This bibliography lists works cited more than once in the Notes, as well as those that have been broadly valuable, even if not specifically cited.

Afflerbach, Holger, "Wilhelm II as Supreme Warlord in the First World War," *War in History* 5, No. 4 (Oct 1998): 427-49.

Beckett, Ian F. W., "French, John Denton Pinkstone, first earl of Ypres (1852–1925)," *Oxford Dictionary of National Biography*, Oxford University Press, 2004; online edn.

Blanning, T. C. W., ed., *The Nineteenth Century: Europe 1789–1914*, The Short Oxford History of Europe (Oxford: Oxford University Press, 2000).

Broadberry, Stephen and Mark Harrison, eds., *The Economics of World War I* (Cambridge: Cambridge University Press, 2005).

—— and Alexander Klein, "Aggregate and Per Capita GDP in Europe, 1870-2000: Continental, Regional and National Data With Changing Boundaries," *Scandinavian Economic History Review* 60, No. 1 (Mar 2012): 79–107, supplementary data.

Bronsart von Schellendorff, Paul and Friedrich, *The Duties of the General Staff*, trans. H. A. Bethell, J. H. V. Crowe, and F. B. Maurice, Fourth ed. (London: His Majesty's Stationary Office, 1905).

Brose, Eric Dorn, *The Kaiser's Army: The Politics of Military Technology in Germany During the Machine Age, 1870–1914* (Oxford: Oxford University Press, 2001).

Bucholz, Arden, *Moltke, Schlieffen, and Prussian War Planning* (New York: Berg, 1991).

Bushnell, John, "The Tsarist Officer Corps, 1881–1914: Customs, Duties, Inefficiency," *The American Historical Review* 86, No. 4 (Oct 1981): 753-80.

Chirot, Daniel, ed., *The Origins of Backwardness in Eastern Europe: Economics and Politics from the Middle Ages Until the Early Twentieth Century* (Berkeley: University of California Press, 1989).

Citino, Robert M., *The German Way of War: From the Thirty Years' War to the Third Reich* (Lawrence, Kansas: University of Kansas Press, 2005).

Clark, Christopher, *Iron Kingdom: The Rise and Downfall of Prussia, 1600–1947* (London: Penguin Books, 2007). Amazon Kindle edition.

——, *Kaiser Wilhelm II* (London: Longman, 2000).

——, *The Sleepwalkers: How Europe Went to War in 1914* (New York: Harper, 2013). Amazon Kindle edition.

Cron, Hermann, *Imperial German Army, 1914–18: Organisation, Structure, Orders of Battle*, trans. C.F. Colton (Solihull, West Midlands: Helion, 1937, 2002). Amazon Kindle edition.

Deák, István, *Beyond Nationalism: A Social and Political History of the Habsburg Officer Corps, 1848–1918* (New York: Oxford University Press, 1990). Amazon Kindle edition.

Donnell, Clayton, *The Forts of the Meuse in World War I* (Botley, Oxford: Osprey, 2007).

Doughty, Robert A., "French Strategy in 1914: Joffre's Own," *Journal of Military History* 67, no. 2 (Apr 2003): 427-54.

——, *Pyrrhic Victory: French Strategy and Operations in the Great War* (Cambridge: Belknap Press of Harvard University Press, 2005).

Echevarria, Antulio J., II, *After Clausewitz: German Military Thinkers Before the Great War* (Lawrence, Kansas: University of Kansas Press, 2000).

Eckermann, Erik, *World History of the Automobile* (Warrendale, Pennsylvania: Society of Automotive Engineers, 2001).

Edmonds, James E., *Military Operations: France and Belgium, 1914, History of the Great War, Based on Official Documents* (London: Macmillan, 1937).

Eloranta, Jari, "From the Great Illusion to the Great War: Military Spending Behaviour of the Great Powers, 1870–1913," *European Review of Economic History* 11, No. 2 (Aug 2007): 255-83.

Evans, Paul W., "Strategic Signal Communication—A Study of Signal Communication as Applied to Large Field Forces, Based Upon the Operations of the German Signal Corps During the March on Paris in 1914," *The* [U.S.] *Signal Corps Bulletin*, No. 82 (Jan-Feb 1935): 24-58.

Ferguson, Niall, "Germany and the Origins of the First World War: New Perspectives," *The Historical Journal* 35, No. 3 (Sep 1992): 725-52.

——, *The Pity of War* (New York: Basic Books, 1998).

——, "Public Finance and National Security: The Domestic Origins of the First World War Revisited," *Past and Present* 142, No. 1 (Feb 1994): 141-68.

Foley, Robert T., ed. & trans., *Alfred von Schlieffen's Military Writings* (London: Cass, 2003).

——, "Preparing the German Army for the First World War: The Operational Ideas of Alfred von Schlieffen and Helmuth von Moltke the Younger," *War and Society* 22, No. 2 (Oct 2004): 1-25.

Förster, Stig, "Dreams and Nightmares: German Military Leadership and the Images of Future Warfare, 1871–1914," in *Anticipating Total War: The German and American Experiences, 1871–1914*, ed. Manfred F. Boemeke and Roger Chickering (Cambridge: Cambridge University Press, 1999).

——, "Facing 'People's War': Moltke the Elder and Germany's Military Options After 1871," *Journal of Strategic Studies* 10, No. 2 (1987): 209-30.

Fuller, William C., Jr., *Strategy and Power in Russia, 1600–1914* (New York: Free Press, 1992).

Gatrell, Peter, *Government, Industry, and Rearmament in Russia, 1900–1914: The Last Argument of Tsarism* (Cambridge: Cambridge University Press, 1994).

Geiss, Imanuel, ed., *July 1914: The Outbeak of the First World War: Selected Documents* (New York: W. W. Norton & Co., 1967).

Geyer, Dietrich, *Russian Imperialism: The Integration of Domestic and Foreign Policy, 1860–1914*, trans. Bruce Little (New Haven: Yale University Press, 1987).

Goodspeed, D. J., *Ludendorff: Genius of World War I* (Boston: Houghton Mifflin, 1966).

Hamilton, Richard F. and Holger H. Herwig, eds., *The Origins of World War I* (Cambridge: Cambridge University Press, 2003), Amazon Kindle edition.

Hansard, *HC Deb 03 August 1914 vol 65 cc1809-32*. Grey's speech to the House of Commons explaining his case for war.

Hastings, Max, *Catastrophe 1914: Europe Goes to War* (New York: Alfred A. Knopf, 2013).

Heal, David, *Victims Nonetheless: The invasion of Luxembourg, 1914* (2010). Amazon Kindle edition.

Herrmann, David G., *The Arming of Europe and the Making of the First World War* (Princeton: Princeton University Press, 1996).

Herwig, Holger H., *The Marne, 1914: The Opening of World War I and the Battle That Changed the World* (New York: Random House, 2009).

Hobson, John M., "The Military-Extraction Gap and the Wary Titan: The Fiscal-Sociology of British Defence Policy 1870–1913," *Journal of European Economic History* 22, No. 3 (Winter 1993): 461-506.

Hogg, Ian V., *The Guns, 1914–18* (New York: Ballantine Books, 1971).

Horne, John and Alan Kramer, *German Atrocities, 1914: A History of Denial* (New Haven, Conn.: Yale University Press, 2002).

Hughes, Daniel J., ed., *Moltke on the Art of War: Selected Writings* (New York: Presidio Press, 1993).

Humphries, Mark Osborne and John Maker, eds., *Germany's Western Front: Translations from the German Official History of the Great War, 1914: Part 1, The Battle of the Frontiers and the Pursuit to the Marne* (Waterloo, Ontario: Wilfrid Laurier University Press, 2013), Amazon Kindle edition.

Hupchick, Dennis P. and Harold E. Cox, *The Palgrave Concise Historical Atlas of the Balkans* (New York: Palgrave, 2001).

Imber, Colin, *The Ottoman Empire, 1300–1650: The Structure of Power* (Basingstoke: Palgrave Macmillan, 2002).

Jäger, Herbert, *German Artillery of World War One* (Marlborough, Wiltshire: Crowood, 2001).

Johnson, Douglas Wilson, *Topography and Strategy in the War* (New York: Holt, 1917).

Kennedy, Paul, "In the Shadow of the Great War," *New York Review of Books* (12 Aug 1999).

——, ed. *The War Plans of the Great Powers, 1890–1914* (Boston: Allen & Unwin, 1979) pp. 222-251. (Originally 1966.)

Kohut, Thomas A., *Wilhelm II and the Germans: A Study in Leadership* (Oxford: Oxford University Press, 1991).

Kuhl, General [Hermann J.] von and General [Walter F. A.] von Bergmann, *Movements and Supply of the German First Army During August and September, 1914* (Fort Leavenworth: Command and General Staff School Press, 1929).

Laux, James M., *The European Automobile Industry* (New York: Twayne Publishers, 1992).

——, "Trucks in the West During the First World War," *Journal of Transport History* 6, No. 2 (Dec 1985): 64-70.

Lieber, Keir A., "The New History of World War I and What It Means for International Relations Theory," *International Security* 32, No. 2 (Fall 2007): 155-91.

Lipkes, Jeff, "Rehearsals: The German Army in Belgium, August 1914: Afterword," http://www.jefflipkes.com/files/Afterwor1.pdf.

——, *Rehearsals: The German Army in Belgium, August 1914* (Leuven, Belgium: Leuven University Press, 2007).

Livesy, Anthony, *The Viking Atlas of World War I* (London: Viking, 1994).

[Ludendorff, Erich F. W.], "General Ludendorff on the German Plan of Campaign, August, 1914," *Field Artillery Journal* 12, No. 2 (Mar-Apr 1922): 126–129.

Ludendorff, [Erich F.W.], ed., *The General Staff and its Problems*, trans. F.A. Holt, 2 vols. (New York: E. P. Dutton & Co., 1920).

MacMillan, Margaret, *The War That Ended Peace: The Road to 1914* (New York: Random House, 2013).

Martel, Gordon, *Origins of the First World War*, Revised 3rd ed. (London: Pearson Longman, 2003). (Provides the text of a number of important documents.)

May, Ernest R., ed. *Knowing One's Enemies: Intelligence Assessment Before the Two World Wars* (Princeton: Princeton University Press, 1984).

Mazower, Mark, *The Balkans: A Short History* (New York: The Modern Library, 2000).

McEvedy, Colin, *The New Penguin Atlas of Recent History: Europe Since 1815* (London: Penguin Books, 2002).

McNeill, William H., *Europe's Steppe Frontier, 1500–1800* (Chicago: University of Chicago Press, 1964).

Military Operations of Belgium: In Defence of the Country, and to Uphold Her Neutrality: The War of 1914. Report compiled by the Commander-in-Chief of the Belgian Army (For the period July 31st to December 31st, 1914) (London: W. H. & L. Collingridge, 1915).

Miller, Steven E., Sean M. Lynn-Jones, and Stephen Van Evera, eds., *Military Strategy and the Origins of the First World War: An International Security Reader*, Revised and Expanded ed. (Princeton: Princeton University Press, 1991).

Millett, Allan R. and Williamson Murray, eds., *Military Effectiveness: Volume I: The First World War* (London: Unwin Hyman, 1988).

Mombauer, Annika, *Helmuth von Moltke and the Origins of the First World War* (Cambridge: Cambridge University Press, 2001).

——, ed. & trans., *The Origins of the First World War: Diplomatic and Military Documents* (Manchester: Manchester University Press, 2013). Includes many recently unearthed documents.

Morrow, John H., Jr., *Building German Airpower, 1909–1914* (Knoxville: University of Tennessee Press, 1976).

——, *The Great War in the Air: Military Aviation from 1909 to 1921* (Washington: Smithsonian Institution Press, 1993).

Noce, Daniel, "Strategic Demolitions of Railroads in Front of the German Right Wing, August-September 1914," (Washington: War Department, Office of the Chief of Engineers, Mar 1940).

Palairet, Michael, *The Balkan Economies, c. 1800–1914: Evolution Without Development* (Cambridge: Cambridge University Press, 1997).

Porch, Douglas, *The March to the Marne: The French Army 1871–1914* (Cambridge: Cambridge University Press, 1981; reprint, 2003).

Quataert, Donald, *The Ottoman Empire, 1700–1922*, 2nd ed. (Cambridge: Cambridge University Press, 2005).

Ralston, David B. , *The Army of the Republic: The Place of the Military in the Political Evolution of France, 1871–1914* (Cambridge: MIT Press, 1967).

Reichsarchiv, *Der Weltkrieg*. See Humphries, Mark Osborne and John Maker, eds.

Ritter, Gerhard, *The Schlieffen Plan: Critique of a Myth* (London: Oswald Wolff, 1958).

Robbins, Keith, "Grey, Edward, Viscount Grey of Fallodon (1862 –1933)", *Oxford Dictionary of National Biography*, Oxford University Press, 2004; online edn, Jan 2011.

Röhl, John C. G., *The Kaiser and His Court: Wilhelm II and the Government of Germany*, trans. Terence F. Cole (Cambridge: Cambridge University Press, 1994).

Romanych, Marc and Martin Rupp, *42cm "Big Bertha" and German Siege Artillery of World War I* (Oxford: Osprey, 2014).

Schlosberg, R[ichard] T., "A Study of the Time Required for Complete Dissemination of Orders of Large Units for Tactical Operations, To the Lowest Echelons, Based Upon Historical Examples of the World War," Individual Research Paper (Fort Leavenworth: Command and General Staff School, 1936).

Schniewindt, General [Rudolph], "Signal Communication Between the Headquarters Staffs During the Warfare of Movement in 1914," *The Signal Corps Bulletin*, No. 74 (Sep-Oct 1933): 1-26.

Senior, Ian, *Home Before the Leaves Fall* (Botley, Oxford: Osprey Publishing, 2012). Amazon Kindle edition.

Showalter, Dennis, "From Deterrence to Doomsday Machine: The German Way of War, 1890–1914," *The Journal of Military History* 64, No. 3 (Jul 2000): 679-710.

Snyder, Jack [L], *Myths of Empire: Domestic Politics and International Ambition* (Ithaca: Cornell University Press, 1991)

—— and Keir A. Lieber, "Correspondence: Defensive Realism and the 'New' History of World War I," *International Security* 33, No. 1 (Summer 2008): 174-94.

Steinberg, Jonathan, *Bismarck: A Life* (Oxford: Oxford University Press, 2011). Amazon Kindle edition.

Stevenson, David, *Armaments and the Coming of War: Europe, 1904–1915* (Oxford: Clarendon Press, 1996).

——, *Cataclysm: The First World War as Political Tragedy* (New York: Basic Books, 2004).

Stone, Norman. *The Eastern Front, 1914–1917* (1975, 2005).

Stoneman, Mark R., *Wilhelm Groener, Officering, and the Schlieffen Plan* (Ph.D. diss., Georgetown University, 2006).

The Times War Atlas and Gazetteer (London: Times Publishing, c. 1916).

Van Creveld, Martin, *Supplying War: Logistics from Wallenstein to Patton* (Cambridge: Cambridge University Press, 1977).

Van Evera, Stephen, "Why Cooperation Failed in 1914," *World Politics* 38, No. 1 (Oct 1985): 80–117.

Wagner, Ray and Heinz Nowarra, *German Combat Planes* (Garden City, New York: Doubleday & Co., 1971).

Wohlforth, William C., "The Perception of Power: Russia in the Pre–1914 Balance," *World Politics* 39, No. 3 (Apr 1987): 353-81.

Zuber, Terence, *The Battle of the Frontiers: Ardennes, 1914* (Stroud, Gloucestershire: The History Press, 2013), Amazon Kindle edition.

——, *German War Planning, 1891–1914: Sources and Interpretations* (Woodbridge, Suffolk: Boydell Press, 2004).

——, *Inventing the Schlieffen Plan: German War Planning 1871–1914* (Oxford: Oxford University Press, 2003).

——, *The Real German War Plan, 1904–1914* (Stroud, Gloucestershire: The History Press, 2011), Amazon Kindle edition.

——, "The 'Schlieffen Plan' and German War Guilt," *War in History* 14, No. 1 (2007): 96–108, p. 96.

——, "The Schlieffen Plan: Fantasy or Catastrophe?" *History Today* 52, No. 9 (Sep 2002): 40-46.

——, "There Never Was a 'Schlieffen Plan': A Reply to Gerhard Gross," *War in History* 17, No. 2 (Apr 2010): 231-49.

——, www.terencezuber.com/schlieffendebate.html.

Glossary of Terms and Abbreviations

BEF	British Expeditionary Force
cannon	Artillery piece able to fire at elevations ranging from horizontal to no more than 50° (usually at high velocity).*
corps	Army formation consisting usually of two divisions (sometimes three) plus additional artillery and supporting troops. In the German Army the standard troop strength of a corps was 42,500 in 1914, with 14,000 horses.
Czar	Also *Tsar*. "Cæsar." The Russian Emperor. (*Czar* can also be used to refer to emperors in other Slavic countries, but is not used so here.)
Dual Monarchy	Austria-Hungary.
field army	Army formation consisting of two or (usually) more corps plus additional heavy artillery and supporting troops.
formation	A higher-level command (generally including division, corps, and field army level) combining units of several different arms or branches under a single commander. Often referred to as a *combined-arms formation* or *command.*
General der Infanterie, or *General der Kavallerie*, or *General der Artillerie.*	German Army rank equivalent to U.S. lieutenant general (three-star). Usual rank for corps command.
Generalleutnant	German Army rank equivalent to U.S. major general (two-star). Usual rank for division command.
Generalmajor	German Army rank equivalent to U.S. brigadier general (one-star).

Generaloberst	German Army rank equivalent to U.S. general (four-star). Usual rank for field army command and higher. (Literally, "colonel general.")
GGS	Great (*i.e.*, central) General Staff of the German Army. In German, *der großer Generalstab.*
Graf	German title of nobility ranking with *count.*
Habsburg	Austro-Hungarian royal family.
Hauptmann	German rank equivalent to U.S. Army captain
howitzer	Artillery piece able to fire at elevations ranging from horizontal to more than 50° (with the intention of delivering high-angle plunging fire).*
Imperial Headquarters	(*Grosse Hauptquartier* or GHQ) The Kaiser and all of the military and civilian officers and officials he needed to exercise his powers of government in war, together with supporting personnel.
Kaiser	"Cæsar." The German Emperor. (*Kaiser* can also be used to refer to emperors in other German-speaking countries, but is not used so here.)
mortar	Artillery piece able to fire at elevations no lower than 45° (at low velocity, for delivering high-angle plunging fire).*
NCO	Noncommissioned officer.
Oberst	German rank equivalent to U.S. Army colonel.
Oberstleutnant	German rank equivalent to U.S. Army lieutenant colonel.
operational level	The level of command decision directing the actions of higher-level formations (field armies, corps, and divisions) in pursuing the overall military objectives.
Supreme Army Headquarters	(*Oberste Heeresleitung* or OHL) The section of Imperial HQ comprising the military personnel who supported the Chief of the General Staff in exercising command over the army on behalf of the Kaiser.

* Definition for the purposes of this book; actual usage varied widely and inconsistently.

Index

Page numbers for illustrations are indicated in *Italic*, those for maps in **bold**, and those for charts and graphs in ***bold Italic***.

16035703R00116

Made in the USA
San Bernardino, CA
15 October 2014